LANGUAGE AND LANGUAGE LEARNING

This Language-Learning Business

LANGUAGE AND LANGUAGE LEARNING

General Editors: RONALD MACKIN *and* PETER STREVENS

This Language-Learning Business

A compilation containing a conversation considerable
correspondence and still more considerable thought
on questions of language and the learning thereof
for the guidance of all those engaged in teaching
or learning that unique subject in the curriculum
a language

HAROLD E. PALMER
and
H. VERE REDMAN

with a biographical essay on
Harold E. Palmer by Dorothée Anderson

London

OXFORD UNIVERSITY PRESS

1969

Oxford University Press, Ely House, London W.1

GLASGOW NEW YORK TORONTO MELBOURNE WELLINGTON
CAPE TOWN SALISBURY IBADAN NAIROBI LUSAKA ADDIS ABABA
BOMBAY CALCUTTA MADRAS KARACHI LAHORE DACCA
KUALA LUMPUR HONG KONG TOKYO

First published by George G. Harrap & Co. Ltd. 1932
First issued in this edition by the Oxford University Press 1969

PRINTED IN GREAT BRITAIN BY HEADLEY BROTHERS LTD.
109 KINGSWAY LONDON WC2 AND ASHFORD KENT

Contents

3 BUSINESS: AN OUTLINE OF A COMPREHENSIVE LANGUAGE COURSE

Editor's Preface

This Language-Learning Business is one of the most readable books in existence on the methodology of language teaching, though the title tells us that the authors view the 'business' from the learner's angle.

Palmer and Redman have collected together just about every current fallacy (current when they wrote the book and, in some quarters, current still) that one can think of concerning linguistic pedagogy, and set about correcting them with rare gusto. There is a sort of panache about their style that is reminiscent of d'Artagnan and his companions.

The book presents, in exemplary fashion, opposing points of view on many fundamental questions about the nature of language and the processes of teaching or acquiring it. This prompts me to suggest that it might well serve as source material for discussion groups or even for formal debates in teacher-training establishments or wherever linguistic studies are an important part of the curriculum. Some sections will lend themselves more easily than others to this kind of exploitation, but these tend to be in any case the most important ones.

Since Palmer and Redman had the lively discussions ('What a racket they made!' said Mrs Palmer later) that led to the writing of this book, much has changed, and many of their then revolutionary suggestions are now part of the new orthodoxy. Where this is so, there is no harm in teachers and students being reminded of the battles that as recently as 1932 had still to be fought and won, and of their debt to these two linguistic musketeers and others like them. And perhaps they will be spurred on to continue fighting for further reform where it is still needed. In the process of discussion they may reach different conclusions from those of our two authors. Very well! So long as they are soundly based, convincingly argued and backed by evidence, they may rest assured that Palmer and Redman would acknowledge their right to differ.

I am deeply indebted to Mrs Dorothée Anderson, who so readily agreed to write a biographical essay on her father to accompany this new edition of *This Language-Learning Business*. With the growing interest in the work of Palmer the linguist and teacher, it is inevitable that readers will wish to know more about Palmer the man. Here, in this short, warm-hearted essay, we have authentic glimpses of him in the many roles he filled in the course of his life, as son, husband, father, scholar, friend, amateur actor ('I am not so much a lecturer,' he once commented to me after a particularly successful and humorous lecture, 'as a light entertainer.'), humanitarian and internationalist . . . and the list is not complete!

Edinburgh, 1968   RONALD MACKIN

Foreword (1932)

The senior partner in this collaboration has been engaged in the learning and teaching of languages and concerned with the problems arising therefrom for a period of thirty years, and the junior partner for a period of ten years. We find on comparing notes of our experiences that, although we have dealt with teachers, learners, and those other self-appointed mentors who do not hesitate to rush in where experts fear to tread, in totally different environments, we have heard in all countries and circumstances the same occasional sense and the same fairly general nonsense talked by all those who are interested in questions of language-teaching or -learning. We have encountered identical resistances, expressed though they have been in diverse ways. We have above all shared a common regret that the problems of linguistic pedagogy have not been considered of sufficient importance to justify a rational codification of them—a codification raised to the level of a science. Surveying the vast amount of knowledge that has been accumulated and inculcated *about* language, we cannot but regret that the equally important subject of how to teach language and how to learn language has been almost totally neglected or left in the hands of quacks on the one hand and fanatics like the present partners on the other. We feel that the poor results in language-learning which educationists the world over periodically deplore are due in no small measure to the fact that linguistic pedagogy has not yet become a respectable science, for it is unreasonable to expect a haphazard and unrecognized science to secure the services of those exponents who alone could make language-teaching what it ought to be.

An attempt has been made in this book first of all to classify the various interpretations of the term 'language', in the belief that one cannot decide how to teach anything until one has first decided what it is that one wishes to teach. Secondly, a classification has been made of the various attitudes towards language possessed by those who wish to learn it, a classification based on our varied experience among pupils of different types and races. Having decided from a careful examination of Part i what a language essentially is, we have attempted to see how best the requirements and resistances expressed in Part 2 can be dealt with without sacrificing what, by examination of Part 1, is believed to be the essential of 'language' to be taught.

Part 3 contains, as it were, the findings based on the two earlier parts. If such and such a thing is a *language* in its essence (as revealed in Part 1), and these are the attitudes of the people to whom we have to teach it (as revealed in Part 2), this is how we should set about it in detail (as revealed in Part 3). We have set down what a number of people understand by a *language*, and deduced from this our own interpretation; we have set down what a number of people understand by *learning* a language, and deduced therefrom our own view of what that process should be; and finally we, whose function it is to guide folk in the process of language-learning, have set out, modestly but unequivocally, to show them what their *business* is, in order that they may achieve satisfactory results.

It will be obvious that if all the germane considerations are to be adequately reviewed a vast amount of mutually contradictory matter must be introduced. It is for this reason that the present form has been chosen. The introductory dialogue shows how we came to realize the necessity for an exact and comprehensive definition of these terms, 'French', 'German', etc., which are bandied about in centres of learning the world over. It was realized that there must be, from the different points of view, a number of interpretations of the term, any one of which might, if adequately expressed, be accepted as complete and final. We knew this to be the case because, let it be confessed, one or the other of us has at some time or another fallen under the spell of each of these interpretations and of the attitude associated with it. We wished, then, to secure the fullest presentation of each case, and consequently we decided upon the series of imaginary letters which makes up Part 1. The views expressed are very often the known opinions of eminent authorities on matters linguistic, but we hasten to add that our letters were conceived not with any idea of parodying the views of such authorities, but merely to clarify our own ideas and, it is to be hoped, those of our readers.

The device of writing an imaginary letter in order to express a real point of view was found so satisfactory in Part 1 that it was used again in Part 2 to express some of the conflicting current attitudes towards language-learning and towards those whose business it is to teach languages.

TOKYO *July 1932*   H. E. P.   H. V. R.

I A Language

INTRODUCTORY: A TYPICAL ADVERTISEMENT, A CONVERSA-
TION ABOUT IT, AND A CIRCULAR LETTER RESULTING FROM
THE CONVERSATION

The University of Timbuctoo has decided to appoint a Professor of English as
from September next. Applicants must have an Honours degree in Modern
Languages from some British university, *etc., etc., etc.*

'The Times', April 6, 1931

H. E. P. I say, Redman, look at this advertisement. What do you make
of it?

H. V. R. If you mean, What sort of man do they want? it depends,
of course, on the students of Timbuctoo. I suppose English is their
native language, isn't it? Or, at any rate, the vehicular language for
their studies?

H. E. P. That's what we don't know. Possibly the Timbuctoo
students, for whose benefit this professor is being sought, have been
brought up in an English-speaking environment, and in matters
linguistic are more or less comparable to English or American children
of the age of seventeen. I suspect, however, that these students know
just as much English as you or I know Latin. I suspect that they have
never once *used* English as a language to think with.

H. V. R. Well, that's what I was just saying; it depends entirely upon
whether English is the vehicular language in the place; it depends
entirely upon whether their environment is such that they have had
occasion to cast their thoughts in the mould provided by the English
language, or whether the English language is for them a strange and
unfamiliar medium of thought-expression. Why not assume for the
moment that the former is the case? Then pretty clearly they want an
authority on English literature.

H. E. P. Why not assume—and the assumption seems to me better
warranted—that the latter is the case? Then pretty clearly they do *not*

want an authority on English literature; and what they do want is someone who knows all about speech psychology and the technique of teaching the most elementary phonetic and semantic mechanisms of English to those who can neither pronounce a *th* nor distinguish between the definite and indefinite articles. Why talk of literature? None are able—or worthy—to approach the heights of English literature who have not made their way across the plains of English as a language. If it is English literature that is required the advertisement would run, 'Professor of English Literature', and not 'Professor of English'.

H. V. R. 'English', I'm afraid, *does* mean 'English literature'—or else it means 'English philology'—in pretty well every university under the sun. It oughtn't to, perhaps, but there it is. You can't get away from it. That's what they mean by 'English' in any university where English is a vehicular language.

H. E. P. But what do they mean by 'English' in universities where English is *not* a vehicular language? I put this question as I would put the question, What do they mean by 'French' or 'Sanskrit' or 'Zulu' in universities where French, Sanskrit, or Zulu is not a vehicular language?

H. V. R. Oh, I see what you're driving at. Of course, you're thinking of Japan, and probably of me. It's funny in a way; it shows the muddle there is in people's minds about what a language is. Take my case for a moment. I teach in two departments of the same institution. One is called the preparatory, and the other the university course. In the preparatory I teach students the language. I try to teach them to speak the language, to write the language, and—if I can—to think in the language. I'm as much a *language* teacher in that preparatory course as I was when I used to teach in the Berlitz School. If I talked about the glories of Shakespeare or the rhythm of Rossetti's sonnets I shouldn't be doing the job; I should be wasting the student's time and my own— I shouldn't be teaching English at all. But in the university department I give lectures on English literature—information about English literature—facts, dates, tendencies, schools, and all the rest of it. (I give these lectures in English, trusting and hoping that my students possess English as a vehicular language to a sufficient extent to have some notion as to what I am driving at—realizing all the time that my knowledge of the subject would carry more weight if I were able to convey it in the terms of the language in which they habitually think— Japanese.) And the authorities insist that I am a teacher of English in both departments. I don't know which is which; but, whichever is which, I'm certainly not in the preparatory department what I am in the university course, but it all goes by the same name.

H. E. P. It wasn't quite that that I was driving at just now. What was more in my mind was this. Every year throughout the world some 20,000 *foreign* students of English who are able to use English as a vehicular language have a more or less keen desire to approach English literature or English philology. These people's desires or requirements are amply catered for. In every university of the world are to be found professors of English literature and philology who have been specially trained to see to it that the desires or requirements of these students are dealt with. Every year five times this number of foreign students, who are able to use English as a vehicular language have a more or less keen desire to approach English commercial correspondence, English economics, or English conversation. The wants of these are so sparsely catered for that some 100,000 foreign students must have recourse to private lessons in some unendowed institution. But let that pass—it is a relatively unimportant point. Relatively unimportant seeing that there are every year fully *twenty million* foreign would-be students of English to whom, by virtue of the fact that they were not born in an English-speaking environment, English is not the (or a) vehicular language. Their need is to learn how to possess English elementarily—as a vehicular language; their need is to come to know the difference between *th* and *s*, between 'a' and 'the', between 'wait' and 'expect', between 'hope' and 'wish', between 'have' and 'be'—even between 'yes' and 'no'.[1] Now these people are not catered for at all—or practically not at all.

H. V. R. Of course, they don't go altogether unprovided for. We happen to have directed our consideration to universities, but the number of universities in any country in the world is very much smaller than the number of secondary schools. And in the secondary schools of non-English-speaking countries English is taught as a language in our own secondary schools, or, at any rate, gestures are made towards it. Of course, that is no argument against the non-continuation of such teaching in the universities, but it does at any rate indicate that some provision, however inadequate, is being made for the people you mention. Though I'm afraid, you know, that even in the secondary schools the literature idea and, even more, the general education idea run

---

[1] Japanese students of university grade frequently use 'yes' for 'no' and vice versa.

away with a lot of the time that might be devoted to effective teaching of the language as such.

H. E. P. That's not surprising when you consider who the teachers are. You say my twenty million are provided for because there are secondary schools with courses in English or French, in which, on your own showing, only a part of the actual time is given to language-teaching as such. But who are the teachers who give the time? Where have they been trained? They have been trained in these universities where they were taught to teach literature and philology. What are their qualifications even for getting such jobs? Degrees in those same universities? It is true that in many English secondary schools a year's residence abroad is required, but what of a knowledge of methodology, speech psychology, or even phonetics? Are they asked for the qualifications possessed by an 'unqualified' teacher in, say, Hugo's Institute? I know, of course, that the Phonetics Department of University College, London, does train English teachers to teach foreign students of English what native English speakers have been taught in the nursery by their mothers, brothers, sisters, playfellows, and nurses (especially on the pronunciation side—less, perhaps, on sides not intimately associated with pronunciation). But where else in the world are English teachers taught to teach those things that in the ordinary course of nature are taught in the nursery?

H. V. R. Pretty well nowhere. For the very good reason that we don't know exactly what really qualifies a person to teach a language, and we can't know that until we know what a language is.

H. E. P. Yes, that's the root of the trouble about this language business. We have no definition either of the term 'language' or of the term 'teaching' or of the term 'learning'. For instance, when did you, an Englishman, start learning English? Was it when you were a few months old, or was it when you first went to school and began learning the ABC? Again, who was your first teacher of English—your mother or the man who first taught you your ABC (as the first step towards literacy and literature)? Now in another branch of learning there happen to be, fortunately, two different and distinct subjects: one's called horticulture and the other's called botany. If by a chance of terminology these two distinct things were both levelled under a common term such as plant-lore we should not know whether we were talking about gardening or about a branch of biology.

H. V. R. Oh, there's a *confusion* all right! But, practically speaking, since at least two things—probably more—are grouped together,

'English' in the curriculum means anything in relation to English which at a given time we don't know. The mother was, of course, the first teacher, the ABC fellow the second—and at the moment the more important. If he'd started on the mother business he'd have been useless and time-wasting. So I say again that a professor of English is required to teach what the students don't know about English. If English is their native language they're assumed to know it for all ordinary purposes, and your professor comes along to tell them all that can be done with English (that is, literature), and all there is to know about English (that is, philology, historical grammar, etc.). And at that time it *is* English to these pupils.

H. E. P. Yes, of course, if it is their native language I quite agree— as every reasonable person must. No professor would dream of carrying on with the mother business with pupils who have spent some years getting English through their parents and playmates. But you're not going to tell me that English is the native language of the people of Timbuctoo. Their present knowledge of English is going to turn out to be far, far more rudimentary than your own knowledge of English was when you were three years old. They have never been through the mother and playmate stage, and if your professor is going to give them Shakespeare or Rossetti it's going to be pearl-casting on a large scale. The professor is going to find himself lecturing on the higher levels of English to hearers who know so little English that they cannot understand—far less use—the very medium with which he expresses himself.

H. V. R. Well, let us suppose that to be more or less true.

H. E. P. But it's absolutely true.

H. V. R. I say 'more or less', because if it were absolutely true they wouldn't require a professor at all—or, at any rate, not a native English professor. You see, the attitude of those responsible for organizing this course in English—whether it's philology or literature—is like this. The lessons—whatever they are—are not aiming at giving the students a practical knowledge of English; they are aiming at giving them a certain measure of liberal culture which comes from the study of literature or philology. That's the attitude. After all, they're studying many other subjects in precisely the same way. Their mathematics in the university will not be commercial arithmetic; there'll be nothing about those mathematics that will be of any use. You can't expect universities to teach English vocationally—or, rather, in a utilitarian spirit—any more than to teach history and mathematics in a utilitarian spirit. If the students want to get something approaching the practical possession of English which I got naturally they'll go to the Berlitz or take a private teacher. Then they'll be taught something. But at present they're just being educated.

H. E. P. Which of the two things, utilitarian English or cultural English, is of more value, would be an interesting subject for debate—and this is the subject you're debating for the moment, while I'm talking about something else. Your analogies show what line of thought you are following up—and it is a side-line. I am not suggesting that we should plant a utilitarian cabbage in our back-garden rather than an artistic—but otherwise useless—carnation, but your analogies suggest that I am. And your analogies are not sound. Commercial arithmetic is not to the higher mathematics what a command of ordinary English is to higher English. The higher mathematics can be approached—and successfully—by those who are ignorant of *commercial* arithmetic, but they cannot be approached by those who are entirely ignorant of arithmetic. The history that the scholar requires may be approached—and successfully—by those who know nothing of the utilitarian history that the politician requires, but it cannot be approached by one who has not an elementary knowledge of chronology. The utilitarian aspect of mathematics or history is not a stepping-stone to the scholarly aspect of mathematics or history. But so far as English is concerned, the practical command of the language *is* the stepping-stone to English literature and philology—more, it is the stuff itself of which literature and philology are composed—unless you would have the Timbuctoo students approach English literature and philology through the medium of the language that they really do possess—the Timbuctoo language. In the whole field of education there is nothing analogous to this language-learning business. It isn't a case of which is more important, the cabbage or the carnation. It's rather a case of which shall we see about first, the cabbage and the carnation or the soil in which we shall subsequently plant either. 'To be or not to be' can be approached only by those who have learned to conjugate the verb 'to be'. I repeat, you are confusing the term 'utilitarian' with the term 'medium of education'.

H. V. R. I suppose there is a tendency in argument to go to extremes, but the language-literature problem is not as simple as you would make out. Oh, I admit your point. Perhaps I *was* a bit off the track; I was thinking more of the relative values of the cabbage and the carnation than of the relative values of the soil and either of them. It's perfectly

obvious that a man who knows no English cannot study English literature except through translations, and if he intends to study it that way—
there's no reason why he shouldn't—the least competent person to
teach him is an Englishman who does not possess the student's language. On the other hand, it's certainly not necessary for your Timbuctoo man to possess English as we possess it to get pleasure, profit, and
real cultivation of the mind from lectures on English literature by an
Englishman. What these university fellows have at the back of their
minds is probably something of this sort. We've got to cultivate our
students' minds: somehow English is a convenient medium, and
teaching in it has the added advantage that in the process the students
will add a little to their practical knowledge of the language.

H. E. P. Oh, I have no doubt whatever that this is what these university fellows have at the back of their minds, but that doesn't help us
much, who have this language-learning business in the front of our
minds. I grant you that your Timbuctoo man may get pleasure, profit,
and all that out of the lectures he listens to, even without possessing
English as you and I possess it, but I can't admit that there will be any
pleasure or profit in these lectures for those who can hardly be said to
possess English at all. But, in order not to go to extremes, I would put
it to you, which of the Timbuctoo students will get the more from
lectures on English literature by the Englishman—those who can
barely follow the spoken word of the lecturer or those who listen to his
words in a manner comparable to that in which the Englishman would
listen to them?

H. V. R. A rhetorical question, that.

H. E. P. Yes, a rhetorical question, with an obvious answer. It is in
proportion as one possesses what you call utilitarian English that one
derives profit from lectures on English literature—for the matter of that,
from English literature itself. Let me give you a concrete example of
what I mean. One of the charms of the literary language is that it
employs the rarer synonyms of those hack words that we work to
death in the ordinary everyday language, but if we are not perfectly
familiar with these hack words in their colloquial setting we cannot get
the charm of their rarer synonyms, What glamour can there be in such
words as 'dawn', 'dusk', 'yesteryear', 'pristine', 'to wend', 'to roam',
'to toll', 'knell', to those who have not been in the habit of using the
common words with which we replace them in our everyday talk? Or,
again, if the Timbuctoo man, for want of knowing better, turns these
words into hack words by using them in trivial contexts, and by so

doing creates Babu English, he will for ever be deaf to the exquisite music and blind to the delicate tone-colour of English poetry.

H. V. R. I quite agree with everything you have said. You have established with a vast quantity of evidence that, in order to appreciate English literature, it is necessary to know English. I think even the people in Timbuctoo agree. But what you haven't established with any notably more remarkable clarity than the Timbuctoo authorities is how much English it is necessary to know before being able to appreciate English literature.

H. E. P. How much English, you ask. I should say broadly the three thousand most colourless and most general words, together with a proportionate number of irregular collocations and the more elementary grammar mechanisms governing their use. This will provide the necessary grounding. Is it not true that every art requires of its votaries a grounding in the elements of that art? To aspire towards a mastery of chess without having spent much time and effort in mechanizing the openings, to aim at a command of the piano without having first attained a reasonable proficiency in fingering, to endeavour to compose English verse without first having enough phonetics to know which words rhyme and which syllables are stressed—all these vain attempts to find short cuts (generally made by those lazy people who proverbially take the most trouble) are comparable to the efforts of those who would approach English literature while English itself is still an un-mastered language.

H. V. R. Yes, I think there's no doubt about that. It's simply a question of confusion of terms. These people have stuck two words together, and because they've been stuck together for a long time we are apt to think they stand for the same thing. What these professors are actually teaching is literature, but they call it English. That's the whole point of Ogden and Richards in their *Meaning of Meaning*;[1] words are only symbols, and as we cannot always determine what they symbolize we quarrel about terms. For instance, there are people who maintain that language *is* literature.

H. E. P. But if language is identical with literature, then literature must be language. What sort of people maintain this? Surely not the professors of literature?

H. V. R. They do, and they don't. Robert Nichols, when he was Professor of English Literature at the Tokyo Imperial University, maintained that language was literature; and his successor, Edmund

[1] Routledge, 1927.

Blunden, held the same thing; and *his* successor, Arundell del Re, was inclined to maintain the same thesis. But I'm jolly well sure that neither Nichols nor Blunden nor del Re would be flattered if they were called 'language teachers'—by which they would be levelled with the teachers in the Oxford Street language schools.[1]

H. E. P. I'm, sure they wouldn't be flattered! Hence, while maintaining that language is literature, they would not go so far as to maintain that literature is language. But there are others who maintain that language has nothing to do with literature, that language is essentially communication.

H. V. R. And that the word 'English' does duty for both 'literature' and 'communication'.

H. E. P. Yes, for both, or perhaps for more than these two things, literature and communication. Others may conceive of English or French or German or Spanish or Italian or Sanskrit or Esperanto or Arabic or Zulu or . . .

H. V. R. Never mind about completing the catalogue! You mean 'a language'.

H. E. P. Well, if *you* don't mind *I* don't mind using the convenient term 'language', to be interpreted as 'English or French or German, etc.' As I was saying, then, others may conceive of language as being something that is neither literature nor communication.

H. V. R. For instance?

H. E. P. For instance—well, let me see—yes, as a *code*, a system of symbols or signals that are not in themselves communication or literature, but may serve as a means of communicating or of composing poetry.

H. V. R. If you come to that a language could be considered as a spelling system.

H. E. P. As a spelling system? Who on earth would ever look upon spelling as having anything to do with the essentials of language?

H. V. R. Judging by the progress—or, rather, the lack of progress— made by spelling-reform, there must be a good many who hold such a view. Really it's amazing; just imagine the processes that are going on at this moment, perhaps. There's the man in Timbuctoo talking about Tennyson; the man in Oxford Street saying, 'This is the pencil'; and some nice Nanny saying, 'C comes long before F, my dear'; another lad saying that all French nouns that end in *ence* are feminine except *silence*; then we have Daniel Jones and Lloyd James telling their

---

[1] This slightly disparaging reference to Oxford Street language schools must not now be taken literally. There are many excellent teachers to be found in them nowadays.—Ed.

foreign students that the *l* in 'let' is 'clear' and the *l* in 'growl' is 'dark', to say nothing of those who are explaining why *accipio* got turned into 'receive', or of those who are discouraging foreign students of English from trying to speak better English than the English themselves (*you* used to be one of the Daniel Jones gang youself, usen't you, Palmer, judging from your *Grammar of Spoken English*?), and those who are explaining the difference between 'pathos' and 'bathos', a metaphor and a simile. All these people are teachers of language—and the people under them all reckon they're learning language.

H. E. P. Just so. If we organized a symposium based on the question, What is this thing called English (or French or German, etc.)? what contradictory and amazing answers we might receive!

H. V. R. Contradictory and amazing no doubt they might be, but none the less they would be most illuminating. And it's a question that ought to be answered. We've been going on for centuries without asking the question, let alone getting an answer to it. Supposing tomorrow we were called upon to found an institute in which to teach English, French, German, etc., what should we teach? There are three hundred and thirty-three Protestant sects in the United States of America, I understand, but they have this one thing in common, their worship of the Spirit of Creation. Surely all these thousand and one Englishes and Frenches, as things to be taught and learned, must have a highest common factor.

H. E. P. Let's try it. Let's first of all draft a letter to some of the people who are known as authorities on French or authorities on German, and say that we want to engage a Professor as head of each of the language departments of this imaginary institute. We can ask these authorities what they understand by the term 'French' or 'German', indicating that on the basis of these interpretations we shall decide what sort of men are best suited for the professorships we have to offer.

H. V. R. Yes, but don't forget the authorities on language too. A fellow like Daniel Jones has the right to a say in a matter of this kind.

H. E. P. And we won't forget the speech-psychology people either. They may not be authorities on *a* language, but they're authorities on *language* all right—at least in one of its most important aspects.

H. V. R. Good!

And this was the letter:

DEAR SIR,

We have been called upon to establish an institute for the teaching of English,

French, German, Spanish, and other languages as foreign languages to students of any age, and we are preoccupied at present with the problem of securing a suitable and adequate staff.

Of course, we realize that there will be a diversity of opinion as to the interpretation of the terms 'English', 'French', etc., and also that, however much we may agree with any one of the narrower interpretations thereof, we shall have to give instruction of various kinds to suit students whose aims and ages will be varied. But we have to engage a head of each department. Are we to get, say, the greatest available authority on French literature, or on French philology, or on French grammar, or on French history, or on the phonetics of French? Or are we rather to get some other sort of man who has an attitude towards the language and a knowledge thereof which transcend all these divisions? If so, what sort of man? To make this decision, we have first to decide what is French, German, etc.? For this reason we are asking you to say what essentially is French, German, etc. In short, what is a language? You will appreciate the fact that we are using here the word 'language' simply as a convenient conventional term by which we avoid a constant use of the term 'English, French, German, Spanish, etc.' On your answer and the answers of our other correspondents, and the conclusions we draw from them, we intend to decide what sort of man shall be the head of each department.

Quite a number of answers were received, but among them six stand out as being mutually exclusive and collectively exhaustive, the remainder being combinations and overlappings of these. The following are the six letters.

LETTER 1. THE LANGUAGE AS A CODE
You ask me what I understand by the term 'a language', explaining at the same time that you are using this term as a convenient synonym for 'English, French, German, Spanish, etc.' What is a language? What is English? What is it that the 'teacher of English' teaches?

This very comprehensive question requires some reflection, for I can imagine many possible answers, some conflicting with the others to a very considerable extent. I can conceive of English as being in its essence a series of combinations of sounds or letters, which combinations make sense. Or I can think of English as being a literature. You say 'English, French, German, Spanish, etc.' If the 'etc.' includes Latin I can even think of a language as being a something that will serve as an instrument for mental discipline, something that may, like mathematics or biology or chess, be utilized to train the youthful mind in habits of observation, of classification, and of ratiocination.

And yet, considering the question from the broadest angle, I am impelled to give what seems to me the broadest answer. English is a *code*, even as French, German, Spanish, Latin, Esperanto, and Ogden's Basic English are codes.

A language is essentially a code—an organized system of signs or signals. It is comparable to the code of maritime signals, in which a series or succession of flags conveys a definite meaning. It is comparable to a commercial code, in which the succession of letters ALFALFAGOB means whatever it does mean. It is comparable to the wireless code, in which SOS stands for 'All hands to the rescue'. It is comparable to the code of bodily gestures, in which the left hand on the other man's shoulder and the right hand in the other man's right hand means 'Come, brother; we understand each other's unspoken thoughts'. A language is comparable to all these things and many more.

When you study a language you study the code that is embodied in it. And its code is set forth and elaborated in its dictionaries—especially those dictionaries that most resemble grammar-books (for instance, the *New English Dictionary*)—and in its grammar-books—especially those grammar-books that most resemble dictionaries (for instance, Mätzner and Poutsma).

A language is codifiable, just as a railway system and service is codifiable in its most complete time-tables. It is codifiable in the way that the compilers of the *New English Dictionary* have codified it. It is also codifiable from a foreign viewpoint and in connexion with a foreign language. The late H. Saito ('the great idiomologist', as he is known by his followers) spent his life in codifying English from the point of view of Japanese.

Palmer, too, in his scheme of what he first called 'ergonics' (and has more latterly called 'mechanism grammar') has done much in the way of codifying English. He starts from simple substitution tables, such as:

I	want	to do it
	wish	
	begin	
	prefer	
	mean	
	etc.	

He then proceeds to the compound type, such as:

I	want	to	do	it
You	wish		see	this
We	begin		take	that
They	prefer		leave	another
The men	mean		write	a few
etc.	etc.		etc.	etc.

and to the complex type, such as:

I	want	to	do	it		
You	wish		see	this		
We	begin		take	that		
They	prefer		etc.	etc.		
The men	mean		go	there		
etc.	etc.		walk	somewhere		
			ride	to London		
			etc.	etc.		
He	wants		give	it	to	him
She	wishes		send	them		them
The man	begins		etc.	etc.		etc.
etc.	etc.					

In his translating machine and automatic sentence-builders he has suggested a method of codification that should be to the foreign student of English what Bradshaw is to the user of the British railway system.

Armed with a railway-guide complete with maps and cross-references, I can find my way anywhere over the railway system of a country. I need not learn the book or even study it; I merely refer to it.

I say I need not learn it, but as I have occasion to use the railway-guide pretty often, as a matter of fact, I do learn it—or, rather, that part of it that concerns the journeys which I have to make.

Moreover, as a prelude to learning the portion of it which I am going to use, or even as a prelude to using it purely consultatively, I learn how to use it—I get the hang of it, as the saying is.

Let's take an example or two. First of all I get the hang of the index, the significations of the stars and circles and triangles and what not which run about the pages. In the early days I frequently forget whether a star means 'Saturdays only' or 'Restaurant car attached'. But after a time I get to know these things, and I can reasonably say that I have got the general hang of the code. Going into the details, I look up the five or six trains which suit me in the morning; from the one that gets me in the neighbourhood of the school early enough for a constitutional up to the last one which makes me miss devotions but begin the first period on time. I look up these things in the first few days—and then I don't; because I've learned them.

I do precisely the same with the five or six trains coming down in the evening, the two or three on Wednesdays and Saturdays, the several that I want to know about for the annual holiday, and so on.

Now, a language can be approached in precisely the same way. If it is sufficiently infallibly codified, as is a railway system, those parts that are required can be easily learned, and other parts can be just as easily added to that original sum of knowledge, if and when required. Now, as every person who is likely to show his face in your institute will wish to learn what it pleases you to call French or German, etc., for an entirely different purpose, it is up to you so to codify this mass of material called French or German, etc., that he can pick out just those portions of it which he requires to learn and also get the hang of the whole thing so that he can find the other portions if and when he requires them. If I have to reach my school at nine o'clock in the morning it's not only useless, but positively exasperating, for my wife to read out of Bradshaw all about the excellent express which leaves my suburb at 10.46. In the same way, if, because you cannot codify your language sufficiently or on other grounds—moral, cultural, educational, etc.—you make your students learn those parts of the language which they don't want to know, you are wasting their time and your own.

But you will answer, 'Any fool can codify a railway system; it is infinitely less complicated, for one thing, and it stays—or, rather, goes—under the orders of half a dozen people who meet together round the board-room table and plan the whole thing out. The trouble with a language is that not half a dozen people decide once and for all where it shall go, but that all the millions of users of that language have their fingers—that is, their tongues or pens—in the pie. And so the code is extremely complicated—and also extremely confused, which explains why the artificial language-makers have got together claiming as much authority as the railway board, and determined to make their language just as simple and infallible as Bradshaw.

Bishop Wilkins started in the seventeenth century with an artificial language—which was also a philosophical language. It could express all human thought with perfect regularity and without anything idiomatic. Three hundred years later came Volapük, Esperanto, Ido, Nov-Esperanto, Latin without Flexions, Occidental, and Novial (to mention only a few), all following on the most approved lines of artificial simplicity exempt from all the style-cramping of the literary tradition. These artificial-language people came to realize that the most perfect language is the one that can be presented in the form of the simplest code. Then comes C. K. Ogden (of the Orthological Institute, Cambridge, England), who produces the most artificial of all artificial languages—Basic English, founded upon the doctrine that the simplest language is that which possesses the minimum vocabulary. On the whole, I am of the opinion that the artificial-language people have a better understanding than have most of the linguistic folk of what constitutes the essentials of a language. Jespersen, the author of *Language : its Nature, Development, and Origin*,[1] the Esperantist, later one of the founders of that artificial language called Ido, still later the creator of Novial, still later the prophet of Interlinguistics—Jespersen is the one who stresses the fact that language is in its essence a *code*, a conventional *code*, a system, a system of signs, an organized code of semantics, which code properly mastered is the key to the study of all languages, artificial or other.

Bishop Wilkins, in my opinion, was a philosophical idealist in this matter of codifying a language. His many successors in their turn held the same ideals. Schleyer, with his Volapük, was an amateur at the job; Zamenhof, the author of Esperanto, was a gifted amateur, but with an insight that was unknown to his predecessors. Couturat and Léau were the first who elevated artificial language to a science, and Jespersen was, and is, their prophet. Jespersen, in his voluminous *Modern English Grammar*,[2] is one of the codifiers of English, and today this Danish professor is looked up to as the veteran and master of the craft of teaching English and all that pertains to English.

For these and other reasons I submit, in answer to your question, that English (or French, or German, or Spanish, etc.—in short, a language) is essentially a *code*—some of these codes being complicated ones and others, notably the artificial ones, being simpler and therefore better.

Language is concerned, I say, with signs, not with the wonders of the *littérateurs*, nor with the blunders of the grammarians or the philologists.

Comments on Letter 1 (In the form of a personal letter)
You have made out an admirable case for language as a code, so much so, indeed, that many will find it convincing. Looking at the thing from this particular angle—and in so doing ignoring the others—it does really seem as if a language were 'essentially a code—an organized system of signs or signals,' as you put it.

[1] Allen and Unwin, 1922.
[2] Allen and Unwin, 1928.

But on examining your claim more closely and more analytically it becomes evident, on your own showing, that it is based not on what language *is*, but on what it ought to be. You say that language is a code, and then prove that it ought to be one by your apotheosis of artificial language. The very simplicity of artificial language is due to the fact that it *can* be codified; the very complexity of natural language is due to the fact that it can't be codified—or, at least, that it can be codified only into a code so complicated as to be useless for practical purposes. So much for your own showing.

But we would go farther and suggest that your chief analogy proves the fallacy of your claim. You compare the language code to the railway code associated with the name of Bradshaw. If the language code is essentially the language, then Bradshaw is essentially the railway, rails, rolling stock, and all—whereas it is evident that the railway is something independent of the railway-guide that tells you how to use it.

Albert Sèchehaye, the chief interpreter of the doctrines of the Geneva school of linguistics (at whose head was de Saussure), compares the language code (which he calls *la langue*) with that aspect of language which is not the code (this he calls *la parole*). He says effectively: The code is to the would-be language-user what the kitchen recipe is to the hungry man; whereas the real thing is to the would-be language-user what the cooked dish is to the hungry man. Just as none can say that food in its essence is the cookery-book, so none can say that a language in its essence is a combination of dictionary and grammar.

You express language as something static, but language is kinetic, if it is anything. It is even more: it is a skill, an art, a *feeling*, and a *doing*, whereas your static code is a potential only. The tubes of paint and the canvas that are sold by Winsor and Newton are static potentialities that may be converted by the skill of the artist into a picture—but they are not the picture. A statue in its essence is not, as has been expressed, a block of marble with all the superfluous parts chiselled off.

You compare the language to Bradshaw, but we would remind you that by the rules set down in Bradshaw the railway system works. This is not the case with a language. A language does not act under orders; it behaves as it will, or as its diversified users will, and the codifiers merely come along and take cognizance of that behaviour. Natural languages are born—not made; but artificial languages and railway systems are made and not born.

Your reference to Professor Jespersen, again, gives the impression that that grand old man of linguistics is, before all, a codifier. A codifier he is—both of natural and of artificial language. But as you have mentioned, he is also the author of that tremendous contribution to linguistics, *Language: its Nature, Development, and Origin*, a book that shows pretty conclusively that language is not a code; and in his ever-popular *How to teach a Foreign Language*[1] he shows that a language is not to be approached as a code.

All luck to the codifiers of languages; may they more and more successfully depict the languages as they are, concretize more and more their abstractions, influenced less and less by the classical traditions that for so long hampered and obstructed constructive, creative, and objective work! But let us not go to the length of proclaiming that their descriptions and tabulations are identical with the things that they are describing and tabulating.

Lastly, we would point out this: that if a language were essentially a code, then those who possess the language best would be those who are the most familiar with the code—and this is not the case. The most brilliant conversationalists, the most eloquent orators, the clearest exponents, the most gifted poets very often turn out to be those who use their language in perfect unconsciousness of the mechanisms by which they produce their effects.

LETTER 2. THE LANGUAGE AS LITERATURE

You ask me what is a language, or, rather, what is French, German, Spanish, English, etc., and explain that you require this interpretation in order that you may decide upon a suitable person to occupy a chair of French or German, etc., in an institute devoted to the teaching of these languages. Your explanation leads me to suppose that what you really wish to know is not so much what a language *is* intrinsically as what it means, what it contains, what it gives—in fact, all the things about it that make it worth learning.

Intrinsically a language is obviously a collection of conventional symbolic sounds and the written signs by which those sounds are represented. But, like the economic commodity, it only acquires *value* in use and in exchange. The *value in use* of a language is its literature, and if it has no value in use it has essentially no value at all, except for purely utilitarian purposes. I take it you are not greatly concerned with the utilitarian purposes of language-learning, for if you

[1] Allen and Unwin, 1904–28.

were you would not be opening an institute on such an extensive scale, for, as you know, the number of people who learn languages for utilitarian purposes—who will ever learn languages for utilitarian purposes—is extremely small.

You are asking, then, what is English, French, German, etc., in terms of a *school*, in terms of *education*. To this my answer can be clear and unequivocal: it is English literature, French literature, etc. The language of any people is embodied and enshrined in its literature. The literature represents the best use to which a people has been able to put its language. Moreover, the literature is the representation of the finest and most valuable thought that a people has been able to evolve. This being the case, it is obvious that it is only this refined product of thought clothed in language which can have any educative value, and therefore it is this which should be taught to the vast number of persons who wish to learn a language simply as a means of culture and education. The educative value of the learning of language purely as language is comparable to the educative value of learning shorthand. Thought is not enriched at all in the process. We learn to express the trivialities, banalities, and mediocrities of one system in the corresponding trivialities, etc., of the other. But let us take a look at the educative value of the study of language as literature.

Each 'thought-word' (or 'thought-locution') that we learn in our own or in any foreign language serves to convey a new thought or to fix a thought of our own or to co-ordinate our own thoughts with the thoughts that others have experienced.

I remember perfectly well how, when young, I had a vague notion, a thought, an idea, that I longed to be able to express; I felt the need of a word with which to express it, but, as I had no word to express it, that thought was in a nebulous, non-articulate state. Then, one day, I heard or read a new word for me—the word 'principle', in the form of some locution such as 'on principle' or 'in principle'. I recognized its thought-content immediately. *This* is the word that I have been wanting; *this* is the word that crystallizes the thought, embodies it, and fixes it. Now I can think more clearly, and I can express to others what has been until now a vague notion, felt but undefined. I can now say (or write) what I have never been able to say (or write) before. I can say (or write), for instance, 'It is not the thing in itself that I object to [or that I admire or support], it is the *principle* of the thing.' Or I am now enabled to say, 'This thing as an isolated instance is not objectionable or admirable or worthy of admiration or detestation, but it is representative of a *principle* that is objectionable or admirable,' etc. So this one word 'principle' served to clarify my thought, to enable me to recognize the thought of another, and to put my thought into communion with the thought of the rest of the thinking world. It was a progress.

This experience has happened to me over and over again. I remember each successive experience, how I hailed with satisfaction and joy each new word or expression that fixed a thought, notion, or concept hitherto vaguely sensed. I remember in this regard such words as 'conventional', 'arbitrary', 'salutary', 'tendency', 'speculative', 'epitomize', *solidarité, tendencieux, capter, samideano, pravulo,* as they were added to my vocabulary.

Later I came to realize that vocabulary has its limits; that there were thoughts, notions, or concepts for which there probably existed no words at all—at least, in the languages with which I was familiar; but that those notions may be concretized in the form not of words as such, but of proverbs, maxims, sayings, etc. How handicapped in thought or philosophy is one who is unacquainted with the proverb 'The burned child dreads the fire', or with the saying 'Love me, love my dog!'

We crystallize and bring to a nucleus our thoughts and notions by means of *words,* and when single words fail us we fall back on proverbs and sayings, and thanks to them we bring ourselves into communion with our fellow-thinkers and -philosophers. And when these fail us we fall back on a further means of thought-crystallization—that provided by classic literature, which provides us with allusions, quotations, and incidents known to the literature of the world. An instrument of thought opens itself up that is unknown to language as language. What single word, simple or compound, can provide us with the means of expressing the thought that is contained in the fable of the Dog in the Manger, in the allusion 'a Pyrrhic victory', or in the quotation 'some fell by the wayside'?

We are tired and exhausted with effort and strivings, we have fought and endured, we can fight and endure no more. Then comes airily, light-heartedly, and critically, one who has not fought in the fight, and makes claim on us for things that we are not prepared to provide or are unwilling to provide—we know not which, for we are weary after the fray—and we answer with heat. What word or collocation or proverb is there in any language that expresses the situation? But Shakespeare gives us an incident that embodies the whole of it, and, knowing the passage, we find the situation to be a familiar one; it crystallizes our thoughts. It is the dialogue between Hotspur and the 'popinjay'.

That is one of the things that literature means for us. It expands our power of thinking and abstraction. Just as the learning of a new word may make our thinking clearer and bring us nearer to the universal community of thought, just as the learning of a new proverb or popular saying may increase our powers of expression, so—and in an infinitely greater measure—will our delving into a classic literature bring us into contact with the great minds that have in all ages and in all places thought the thoughts that all must think who are able to think, who are worthy to think.

One speaks tritely of 'thinking in English' (or French, or whatever the language may be) and claims that the language (whichever it is) is the instrument of thought, the thing that you think with. But in using the term 'thinking in English' (etc.), do we sufficiently emphasize the *quality* of the thought? 'Let us teach our students to think in English' (etc.), says the teacher, and then he proceeds to cause his students to think such trivial thoughts as 'This is a pencil and not a blackboard', as 'An elephant is larger than a mouse', or as 'Without ears we cannot hear'; whereas what he should be doing is to cause his students to think thoughts of which we might say, 'These are thoughts that they could not have thought without the study of the language of that thinker who first thought the thoughts, and who, in thinking them and embodying them in thought-situations, enriched the contents of a literature, and by doing so made the language of that literature more worth learning.'

I want also to remind you that just as a language is essentially its literature, so it is its best forms—that is to say, its literary forms—which should be taught. You will answer that you do not know what are its best forms, that the acclaimed masters of literature are often in contradiction the one with the other on this point. As a matter of fact, there are also no fixed standards of decent behaviour, no fixed standards of respectable attire, but most of us recognize the bounder when we see him, and, moreover, he is apt to continue to bound even after ingeniously (for bounders are usually ingenious) he has codified the conventions of decent society and learned the code. He goes on bounding because he has no experience of proper behaviour, because he has not practised it, because he has not lived long enough in its atmosphere. Now literary language, good English, good French, etc., is like good manners—a thing which cannot be exactly defined, but which can be acquired by mixing in the society of the masters of good English and good French, etc. And so, although Shakespeare occasionally puts a singular verb with a plural subject and Carlyle scatters capitals, colons, and commas in a liberal fashion, these writers are sounder guides to good English than some manual which has carefully collected all the slipshod expressions of the so-called 'current language'.

Therefore I say to you that there *is* such a thing as good English or good French. Good language is the language of those who are constantly in contact with the language's soul, its literature. And if there is such a thing as good language there is also such a thing as bad language (quite apart from oaths). This bad language is admittedly in use—I sometimes use it myself—but I use it knowing it to be bad, and I do not suppose that by using it I am going to turn it into good language. A language changes, as manners change, but bad manners never become good, nor does bad language become good language. 'But', you will say, 'there are so many borderline cases, how are we to define for our students what is good?' I answer this again with the metaphor of manners. Keep your students in decent society, the society of the best writers, so that they may almost unconsciously form their own standards, and you will not have the trouble to define what is meant by good language.

Moreover, I do hope that you will not stress too much the importance of phonetics, for as I see it phonetics has very little to do with language. Phonetics is the science of sound-abstraction and vocal physiology. But neither of these things has very much to do with this great record of man's experience, aspirations, and meditation which is literature— literature, as I have said, the soul of language. I can quite admit that your sound abstractions are useful to persons learning a foreign language, in getting that approximation to the native pronunciation which is not only desirable but necessary. But there the utility of phonetics to the average person ends. There is not the slightest advantage in a further study of the subject; in fact, as far as appreciation of literature goes, it is definitely harmful. It will train the ear to catch isolated sounds and to miss melodies. Aesthetic pleasure will be lost in scientific observation, and the mind will play on the sound of words instead of on their colour and their thought.

The phoneticians make one great mistake, a mistake which is shared by many, including the grammarians, in supposing that a language is a science. Now a dead language is a science—that's why it is dead—

or rather it is a science because it is dead. Because it is dead it can be pinned down, its form and structure analysed, its sounds clearly defined. But a living language or a living literature cannot be so pinned down. It refuses to 'stay put' either as to sound or sense. By insistence on phonetics, then, you are making students learn what a few people thought the language sounded like the year before last.

Let me in a final paragraph sum up what I have said. Language as something to be learned is essentially literature; literature which enables the learner not only to express new thoughts, but to crystallize old and vague ones. This being the case, it is to be urged that throughout language instruction care should be taken to use models of literary language almost exclusively, my contention being that this is the only language worth learning for any purposes other than the most strictly utilitarian. Lastly, I urge that, since the conception of language as essentially successions of sounds is inaccurate in itself, and since it leads the attention of the learner away from what *is* essential in language, preoccupation with mere phonetics should be reduced to a minimum.

In view of these considerations I think that the best head of each department of your institute would be an authority on the native literature.

Comments on Letter 2

This answer is very typical of the opinions of one who is really viewing language not as a foreigner but as a native. The native at the age of twelve finds himself in possession of a vast quantity of language; to his conscious knowledge he hasn't learned it at all. At the same time he is aware of a capacity to learn things, and he begins to learn things— even things in relation to this vast quantity of knowledge. He learns a number of things *about* the knowledge he possesses: that these words that he uses, for example, were once written in a different way; and that they are combined in certain ways, with which he is perfectly familiar, according to certain rules. In addition he learns what can be done with the knowledge he possesses; how it can be improved upon, and, when improved upon, how his mind is enriched both by attempts so to use it and by the experience of contact with the achievements of the acknowledged masters of its use. He takes in all this knowledge with considerable effort and profit; he has learned it all— one might even say he has earned it all, earned it by the efforts of concentration in the classroom and study. And very naturally his attitude

towards his hard-earned possessions is much more respectful than that
towards his inherited possessions.

The foreigner, on the other hand, approaching a language, must do
studially what the native has done spontaneously, and that is not
something which can be done in half an hour; it represents the accumulated absorption of linguistic phenomena of a good many years.
Either our correspondent is forgetting this or else—which is much more
probable—he is suggesting that this, the first phase of natural language
study, should be skipped. He is suggesting that it should be skipped
because he conceives it as involving processes that are not educative,
and he is assuming that they are not educative in the case of the
foreigner because they were not educative in the case of the native. It
is this point that makes the letter typical of all the ill-informed thought
and expression on the problems of language-teaching to which we have
been treated for the past four hundred years. Of all the fallacies concerned with language and language-study this one stands out pre-
eminently: the fallacy *that the first phase of natural language-study may be
ignored when the language is a foreign one.*

If our correspondent would have us ignore the first phase on the
grounds that one cannot learn studially what in the case of one's own
language is absorbed intuitively, we should only have to explain to
him the methods that could be employed, and in many schools nowadays are being employed, to do just that thing. But our lover of literature appears to base his resistance to this first-phase teaching on the
grounds that the processes involved are not educative in the general
sense. Now this contention is based on another confusion. The *disciplines*
of language-learning are different from those employed in the learning
of any other kind of subject, but this does not necessarily mean that
they are inferior from an educational point of view. The very feeling
that they are inferior emanates, as we have said, from the fact that, in
the case of the native, what these disciplines set out to inculcate has
been acquired without conscious effort. The language teachers of
another generation, realizing this, but not wishing—as our correspondent appears to wish—to skip altogether the first phase, tried to bring
into language-teaching the conventional technique of education by
presenting language as a science, with grammar and syntax as its
principles and rules. In this way they succeeded in persuading themselves and their pupils that what was being done was infinitely more
educative than merely enabling an adolescent to reach an approximation to the capacity possessed by the foreign child. Modern teachers of

languages, having been shown by experience that these so-called educative methods did not achieve the desired results, have sought a closer approximation to the processes through which the foreign child passes, and are seeking to cause their students to pass through those processes consciously. The instruction given involves such disciplines as observation, imitation, use of analogy, promptness in reaction to speech stimuli, etc.—disciplines which the teachers using them justly claim to be as educative as any of the conventional disciplines, and which, incidentally, are productive of efficiency in the subject in question.

Our correspondent has said that the only thing worth learning in a language is its literature, and we have shown that, quite apart from actual linguistic efficiency, there are immense intellectual advantages in the mere learning of language as such. Moreover, our friend must realize that the approach to literature is through language, and that the power to learn a foreign literature depends almost entirely on the degree with which one is familiar with the language in which it is written. Until you know a language in a manner comparable to that of the native, it is better to confine your studies of that foreign literature to translations and commentaries. As Mr H. O. Coleman puts it in his contribution to *Modernism in Language Teaching*:[1]

There is exalted, remote literature, and there is simple literature, more akin to ordinary speech. How can we feel anything about this difference, unless we first have a knowledge of ordinary speech as a basis for comparison? There is literature which is stiff and bad, because it is too remote from ordinary speech for the subject in hand; there is literature that is too ordinary, too conversational for the serious subject dealt with. How can we apply such criticisms until we are familiar with the ordinary language of conversation? The words *courroux* and *forfait* in Racine, with their recurrent, solemn effect, are lost on anyone to whom the words *colère* and *crime* are not the natural words for the things indicated.

The value of literature is not questioned for a moment, and in the foregoing section we have merely sought to show how the learner's approach to it may be made easier and more comprehensive by a thorough study of ordinary language. Exactly the same applies to that section of our

[1] Edited by H. E. Moore (Heffer, 1925).

correspondent's letter which refers to the extension of thought and the crystallization of thought which literature furnishes. Literature has these qualities, but they can only be appreciated and thus furnish their full value when they are seen in relation to the ordinary background of language knowledge. Literary allusions are indeed in a certain measure a language of the cultured, yet they are a language not apart from plain language, but built around plain language. They enable the cultured the world over to understand one another *à demi-mot*, but understanding *à demi-mot* does not precede, it follows, understanding *à mot entier*. We have to prepare our students to appreciate literature, and the preparation is a long and rather arduous one. What our friend is proposing is a short-cut—he is advocating an attempt to give our students superficial knowledge—but superficiality is against all the best traditions of the field of humanistic culture which he represents. In other fields his proposals could be called cheap-jack; we prefer to call them simply misguided.

We are not impressed as much as we ought to be by the 'good manners, good society' simile. Our correspondent bids us keep our students in mannerly society as far as language is concerned rather than in unmannerly society. He seems to suppose that every action in our daily life is either mannerly or unmannerly, and to extend this arbitrarily comprehensive division of human activities to the field of language. Every phrase, then, even every word, is somehow either good or bad, and we are to inculcate the one and eschew the other. Now this is egregious nonsense in our relations with our fellow-men; it is possibly still more absurd in relation to language. Literature is the product of language-users on their best behaviour, on their Court behaviour; and in actual fact it is only to monarchs and minions that Court behaviour is in any sense normal—and, after all, unless good behaviour is normal it is not worth a moment's consideration. A man who is courtly on the football-field is as much an outsider as is the man who calls out 'Well done, George!' in the House of Lords when His Majesty delivers the King's Speech. If, then, we are to keep our student in constant contact with party manners we are going to make of him as much of a linguistic bounder as if we taught him every trivial vulgarism that the language contains. In addition to making him a bounder we are also going to make him a Babu, mixing Wildean brilliance with Ruskinian verbosity, Shakespearean obscenity with Arnold-like purity; not a man fit for decent society or, for the matter of that, for indecent society, but one fit for no society at all.

Professor H. C. Wyld has said:

Nothing is more mistaken than the view which is sometimes taught, that the colloquial style is less 'correct' than that of books, and that such contractions, for instance, as *isn't, can't, they're* (they are), *I've, he'll,* and hundreds of others which are habitual to all good speakers of English, are in reality vulgarisms, which 'correct' speakers should avoid. The fact is, that these forms are in many cases the *only* 'correct' forms in colloquial speech, and to use *is not, they are, he will,* and so on, would be pedantic or worse, if that be possible.

We have dealt with this comparison at some length simply because its absurdity is so tempting, but in reality we might have said from the start that in language, as in life, what is very good, like what is very bad, plays a small and superficial part. Outside those two limited spheres of questionable and elegant language lies the infinitely greater sphere of language which is neither questionable nor elegant. That obviously is the language we have to teach. There is inevitably a period preceding that which determines good or bad manners—a period in which manners are neither those of the bounder nor those of the perfect social product, in which they are simply absent or rudimentary. Before learning to live in manner mannerly the child has to learn to live *tout court.* In language also before learning to speak or write in manner literary we would have our students learn simply to *speak* or *write.* It is in the primary business of *using* a language that we must train our students before training them to use it, or even to appreciate it, *elegantly*; and we maintain that by so doing, when the time comes, they will appreciate much more clearly how to use and how to recognize a language's refinements. We do not propose to teach them at the age of four that port is served with dessert or that the sherry with the soup comes in flute-like glasses (only in England, by the way!). We shall tell them rather, like the conscientious mentors that we are, that both port and sherry are inventions of the devil (that is to say, the *littérateur*), not because we really think so, but lest in their inexperience they put port in the sherry glasses and serve it as a cocktail and spoil their own and their guests' (that is to say, their hearers') digestion. In a word, we are going to teach the essentials of language as the child is taught the essentials of living, believing that every refinement must be superimposed on a solid foundation.

We are advised to beware of phonetics (1) because phonetics is not essentially language, and (2) because preoccupation with phonetics leads the student's attention away from the beauties of language. We could understand such a preposterous thesis being maintained by one who regarded language merely as oral communication, but from one who is concerned so much with literature it seems almost incredible. What is the highest form of literature? Is it not poetry? What is the essential quality of poetry? Is it not the synthesis of sound and sense? Is it not the expression of sense through sound? Is not, then, mispronounced poetry ruined poetry—and therefore valueless poetry? And yet we are told that we are to restrict as far as possible our efforts to give to our students the power to recognize and to reproduce accurately the sounds of a language, and we are told it by the same person who bids us keep our students in contact throughout all their studies with Shakespeare, who wrote in prose, 'Speak the speech, I pray you, as I pronounced it to you, trippingly on the tongue: but if you mouth it, as many of your players do, I had as lief the town-crier spoke my lines.'

We shall teach the thoery and notation of phonetics to our students of language for the same reason as that for which the teacher of the violin teaches the theory and notation of music. We know that violin-playing is something apart from the theory and notation of music, and yet we recognize that this theory and notation constitutes one of the most useful aids to violin-playing. For phonetic theory and notation is an aid not only to utilitarian English, but also—perhaps in a greater degree—to language as literature.

Quite by the way, we cannot but feel somewhat astonished that the writer who is so much concerned with good English forms is for some reason disdainful of good English sounds. It is almost like one who suggests that you must behave yourself beautifully in the dining-room, but that you can do whatever you like—in fact, should be encouraged to do whatever you like—when you get into the drawing-room. Our correspondent admits that phonetics is an aid to good pronunciation, but he does not insist that our students should be kept in good pronunciation society—as far as pronunciation is concerned, they are to be allowed to run the streets. He makes as much play with the diversity of pronunciation as we have done with the diversity of linguistic good form, but he does not see, as we have seen, that outside the two limited spheres of objectionable pronunciation and elegant pronunciation there is the infinitely greater sphere of pronunciation that is neither elegant nor objectionable, but simply normal—and therefore good.

He has perhaps not had the opportunities to see, as we have seen, that the pronunciation of the average foreigner is neither elegant nor objectionable—but simply unintelligible or barely intelligible. In order to train our students in the acquirement and retention of that normal pronunciation, we must give them an aid to recognition and reproduction of the sounds of the language they are learning, not only as individual sounds considered analytically, but also as successions of sounds, considered synthetically, with all their attributes of weakening, assimilation, stress, and intonation.

We know what our correspondent will say to all this: 'What is the aim of your preoccupation with correct pronunciation? Is it merely to understand the utterance of the native and to be intelligible when you speak the foreign language? If so you are forgetting that the large majority of language learners the world over need never do the one or the other.' We answer his question with an emphatic negative. The sound element in a language is as much a part of the spirit of that language as is its syntax or its prosody. It is because we do not know or we do not feel the sound element in Latin or Greek that their spirit often evades us, and Cicero in quality of mind appears to our imagination something like an Oxford don, something indeed, like *the* particular Oxford don from whose lips we first heard the reconstructed sounds of the great Roman's prose. It is not in poetry alone that sound is an aid to sense, but in all our dealings with a language, if we are to get its spirit. That is to say, to get from a language its greatest educational and cultural value we must associate with its written forms the sounds that are behind them.

LETTER 3. THE LANGUAGE AS CONVERSATION

Looking at English, French, German, etc., broadly, uninfluenced either by doctrinaires and those who have devised complicated (if ingenious) 'methods' of learning languages, or by the complicated (if scientific) theories of the speech-psychologists, I am inclined to say that language is based on—and is an extension of—*conversation.*

In the same way that all language originated in conversation, each one of us approached our mother tongue as conversation. In the same way that languages were spoken thousands of years before ever they were written, so each of us spoke our mother tongue some years before we learned to read or to speak it. And we spoke and understood it not as the medium of philosophical or technical thought, not as the medium of oratory or rhetoric, not as a series of mental gymnastics, not as a training in the humanities or the classics, but as the medium of everyday intercourse.

That this is true is borne out in practice, as I hope to show in the following pages.

We may say that we are ignorant of this or that foreign language, but nevertheless we sometimes find, on reflection, that we are not entirely ignorant of that language. What words and expressions are there that we do know?

Who, ignorant of French, does not at least know such expressions as the following:

Bonjour, monsieur.
Bonsoir, madame.
Comment vous portez-vous, mademoiselle?
S'il vous plaît.
Merci.
Au revoir.

Or, ignorant of German, such expressions as:

Guten Tag.
Bitte.
Danke schön.
Ach, mein Gott!
Auf Wiedersehen!

Most foreigners ignorant of English seem to know at least:

How do you do?
All right.
Oh, yes.
Very well.
Thank you.

Other examples:

Salaam, Baksheesh (*Arabic* or *Near East*).
Mañana, Buenas noches, Carramba (*Spanish*).
Skol! (*Scandinavian*).
Ohio (*Japanese*).
Begorrah (*Irish*).
Attaboy (*American*).

In short, the few expressions that we do know turn out almost invariably to be relatively polite expressions, greetings, and conversational openings.

We have it on the authority of Sweet[1] that the study of a foreign language must start with the conversational: 'Everything therefore points to the conclusion that in learning foreign languages we should follow the natural order in which we learn our own language: that is that we should begin with learning the spoken language.'

H. C. Wyld, the authority on the origin of dialect, shows indirectly in *A History of Modern Colloquial English*[2] that the colloquial is the essence of the language.

H. L. Mencken, in his *American Language*,[3] has come to the same conclusion. In this richly documented work he points to the periodical quickenings of an otherwise moribund language by means of a frank recognition of the spontaneous creativeness of the conversationalists.

It is constantly asserted, not only by the old school, but also by the new—for example, by Mr Kittson and the late Mr Hardress O'Grady—that the chief object of our study of a foreign language is to appreciate its literature. This I flatly deny. Taking literature in its widest sense, as language used for an aesthetic purpose (in which sense even unlettered races have quite definite literary language), I assert unhesitatingly that literature is not the object of our study. Our object is not to understand what is noble and beautiful in the foreigner, but all that is in him, good, bad, or indifferent.

Language is a living thing, and must be approached as a living thing. This is, of course, a cheap truism, but is true in spite of its triteness. What is really behind this truism is this fact that I am stressing with such insistence: that language as a living thing is language as conversation.

All language is based ultimately on that form of it that we use spontaneously and naturally when we are speaking it, or listening to it, with a perfect unconsciousness of its traditional or classic form.

Those who possess a foreign language (in the best sense of the verb 'to possess') are those who have a perfect command of the language as actually used in conversation. We say of one, 'He has an idiomatic command of the language,' and this is the highest compliment we can pay him in the sphere of linguistics.

[1] *The Practical Study of Languages.* Reprinted Oxford University Press, 1964, p. 51.
[2] Fisher Unwin, 1920.
[3] Knopf, 1919.

A Frenchman or a Russian says to an Englishman, 'That is the person to whom I am referring.' The Englishman admires this elegant mode of expression, and may observe that the user speaks English better than an Englishman.

Another Frenchman or Russian (or maybe a Pole or a Turk or a Chinese) in the same circumstances says, 'That's the man I'm talking about.' This same foreigner on other occasions expresses himself in such ways as, 'But, my dear man, hang it all, I've simply *got* to do it', or 'It's a frightful nuisance, and all that, you know, but, damn it all, one has to draw the line somewhere, what?' or 'If anyone comes tell them I'm busy', or 'Nobody likes to be told that they are utterly inartistic' (in imitation of His Royal Highness the Duke of Gloucester, who, being the King's son, naturally uses the 'King's English'—that is, conversational English.)[1] Instead of the correct 'This sort of people', 'It is I', 'Tomorrow will be Friday', 'Not so far as', 'I saw him only yesterday', and 'Try to come tomorrow', he says, 'These sort of people', 'It's me', 'Tomorrow's Friday', 'Not as far as', 'I only saw him yesterday', and 'Try and come tomorrow'.

In these and many other ways this Frenchman or Russian (or maybe a Pole or a Turk or a Chinese) offends against the canons of classical English. The Englishman does not admire such modes of expression, but nevertheless pays the greatest of all compliments when he remarks that this foreigner speaks English just as the English do themselves.

I am reminded here of a *Punch* joke. Two English sailors are commenting on the degree of perfection in which some foreign shipmate possesses English: 'Ee's a Hitalian bloke, but lumme, 'ee speaks puffick Hinglish just like wot you an' me does.'

'Not to speak better English than the Englishman does'; 'To use French just as the average Frenchman does'; 'To possess German as does the native educated German—no better, no worse'; 'To speak the foreign language so colloquially that one might be taken for a native'; 'To disregard the canons of classical Castilian to such an extent that one might pass for a Spaniard'; these are among the ideals of linguistic attainment as set forth by those who, with Sweet, Wyld, Passy, Jones, Mencken, Coleman, and Palmer, maintain—and rightly— that the language in its essence is the present-day colloquial form of that language.

[1] This sentence is a quotation from the reply of His Royal Highness the Duke of Gloucester to the loyal toast on the occasion of the Royal Academy banquet, May 2, 1931.

English (French, etc.) is the sort of thing that English (French, etc.) people use when they are not on their best, but on their ordinary, behaviour—nothing more, nothing less.

Language contains all the elements of democracy. It cannot be imposed from on high; it can only be imposed by majorities; and, above all, its government, like that of all democracies, is government by *talking*. I hope you will keep this particularly in mind, and, in order that you may do so, I am sending you a tastefully illuminated motto which I recommend you to hang in some conspicuous place where the pious are wont to hang texts. You'll see that it is LANGUAGE IS GOVERNED BY TALKING. This is a fundamental fact which neither your students nor your teachers should be allowed to forget.

Comments on Letter 3. (In the form of a personal letter)
In answer to our question you say that a language is essentially conversation, and you would, we take it, recommend us to engage as the head of each language department a native speaker of that language, endowed with a capacity to collect and classify the spoken varieties of the language as distinct from the written varieties, which, as you say—probably rightly—always lag behind the spoken word.

In a number of examples you show very clearly that the conversational usage of the average educated Frenchman (or Englishman) differs very much from his usage in writing. You claim, and again probably rightly, that the spoken usage of today will be the written usage of tomorrow. But as 'French' or 'English' must include both the written and the spoken usage, the student who becomes proficient in the one is, on your showing, likely to be deficient in the other. It is quite useless to point out to him that what he speaks now will be of value to him when writing in, say, ten years' time. He wants to speak and to write *now*. There is no doubt that dress-clothes, with their board shirts and stiff collars, bear a closer relation to the clothes of the past than do the softer and more comfortable garments of our day-time wear. There is no doubt that the more modern and more comfortable day-time wear will influence and is influencing the more ceremonial attire for the evening. Nevertheless, at the present time a man who wears a soft collar at an evening party is as out of place as one in swallow-tails at the office. In the same way the written language is an older thing—it is a ceremonial thing—but it exists and it can no more be disregarded than can the spoken language, the necessity for which you have so ably urged.

In a word, then, you have not told us what a language is; you have
told us only what you consider to be a very important aspect of it.
The French of an educated Frenchman is not only the French which
he speaks, it is also the French which he writes. The French which he
possesses and which we must teach is something which contains those
two. It is true that Sweet asserts that language-study must start with
the colloquial, but he says *start* and not *remain*. He says in effect that
we cannot run before we can walk, but he does not suggest that we
must never run at all.

When you become enthusiastic about the Frenchman who speaks
English, with his 'Hang it all' and 'What I mean to say', you forget
that this again is a specialist acquirement—a jargon—which changes
from year to year, even from day to day. His easy colloquial of today
may be the stilted or the ludicrous of tomorrow. Surely a language is
essentially something more than a jargon at the mercy of quickly
changing fashions. English, for example, as an entity, a unity, has
existed for nearly six hundred years. 'Conversation' has completely
changed at least a dozen times in that period, but 'English' has always
been there. There is some sort of essential English which might have
been taught in Chaucer's time and which would be perfectly good
today. It wasn't 'conversation', and it most certainly wasn't 'written
English'. What was it? We aim at defining, not an 'English' which will
last six hundred years, but simply one that will last a lifetime—the
lifetime of our students. That is the English or French we want to
teach our students, and which we want our professor to know and to
know how to teach.

LETTER 4. THE LANGUAGE AS COMMUNICATION
Looking at a language (duly defined as 'English, French, German,
etc.') from the broadest possible angle, we can only describe it in its
essence as *a means of communication.*

Teachers of languages, including all varieties ranging from that
poor hack, the language-teacher, to one who holds a chair of, say,
English in some university (at home or abroad), generally miss this
fundamental point. They look upon the language as a *code* or as a
subject or as a *literature*—in short as something to be learned or studied,
whereas a language is rather something to be *used*.

All these teachers stress unduly the element of accuracy—they are for ever striving to prevent their pupils from making what they call mistakes in grammar, vocabulary, pronunciation, or spelling; or correcting such mistakes when they occur. They judge of their pupil's degree of success only in terms of the degree of accuracy in his compositions, translations, or conversation. They will have their pupils conform to a model, to some standard. Their work is normative—and consequently negative. 'Don't say this.' 'Don't write that.' 'Avoid this form.' 'That is bad grammar.' 'This is not colloquial.' 'That is not elegant.' That is the burden of their teaching. All because they fail to grasp the fact that language is in its essence nothing other than a series of acts of communication.

Now the ideal approach to a language as means of communication occurs when two people, speaking mutually unintelligible languages, come together in circumstances necessitating communication. Using either of the languages—or both—they soon come to be able to communicate successfully. They do not worry about accuracy or conformity to any recognized code—they simply go ahead, and, aided by gestures and gesticulations, come to understand the ideas that each is striving to convey.

Look at the British soldier in France making his wants known to the French farmer's wife. 'Oofs?' inquires the British Tommy (meaning 'Have you any eggs?'). 'Ooofs nahpoo,' answers Madame (successfully conveying the information that there are no eggs).

Look at Robinson Crusoe and Man Friday. Listen to Man Friday, when he says, 'O master! O master! O sorrow! O bad! . . . O—yonder—there; . . . one, two, three canoe! one, two, three!' Robinson Crusoe understood perfectly, as you or I would have understood. Robinson Crusoe did not answer '*Canoes*, Friday, *canoes*, not *canoe*. On your own showing there is more than one canoe, and therefore we must add to the word *canoe* the sign of the plural, an *s*, here pronounced as *z*.' He simply answered, 'Well Friday, do not be frighted . . . We must resolve to fight them.' And, to my mind, to correct Friday's Caribbean English is as uncalled for as it is to correct Robinson Crusoe's 'frighted' into 'frightened'.

Listen to the mother and her baby. 'Baby go tata?' suggests the latter. 'Yes, Baby go tat in ikkle pram-pram with Nana.'

An English lecturer on the Law of Torts at a foreign university told me recently that his pupils were so exceptionally bright that it was almost impossible to fail any of them at examinations. 'Their papers,' he said, 'average about eighty marks out of a hundred.' I thought this remarkable, for most teachers of English in that country complain that their pupils are so dull that it is almost impossible to pass any but an insignificant handful at examinations. I therefore inquired, 'How is it that their English composition is so exceptionally good?'

'English composition exceptionally good!' he echoed. 'It's nothing of the sort; as composition it is beneath contempt. There are few sentences without more than one mistake in number, article, tense, spelling, and syntax.'

'Then is it their pronunciation that is so remarkably good?' I inquired further.

'Their English pronunciation is exceptionally bad,' he answered. 'It is their knowledge of the Law of Torts that is exceptionally good. These students follow my lectures with attention; they understand the various points that I discuss before them, and they show in their examination papers that they have an uncommonly good grasp of the subject. You don't think that I would deduct points because of mistakes in spelling, grammar, or pronunciation. Why should I? It is enough for me that they understand what I say and I understand what they write.'

Now this, I maintain, is the right attitude to take. All this codifying of languages according to conventional standards is beside the point.

Let me give you an example of what I mean:

Look you here, listen a little.

Listen my words, if they are not true, yes?

I tell this to you, saying that language business is all communication. No more. Sufficient, yes? You do agree? I am thinking so. Grammar-like things and the pronunciation, also without mention of the spelling, it isn't false if we tell: these are innowise true essence of language, but only simply accident-like not of import.

This is my ideas *re* this subject that you will that I tell to you concerning.

Now the grammarian and the academician and the technician and the schoolmaster and the professor may all say what they will, but I maintain that the above is English, and that it is good English in the measure that it conveys ideas in an intelligible manner. Shakespeare, I am willing to admit, did not write like that; that is why Shakespeare is generally unintelligible. Fowler does not write like that, either, but if we followed his advice we should have to study our own language for fifty years before daring to use it as a medium of communication.

Let us suppose, again, that an English student of economics is desirous of becoming acquainted with the thought-content of a book on economics written in French. What does he care for the nature of French as a code, its grammatical conventions, its pronunciation, or its spelling? If he is bothered with these things he will give up his intention of reading the book. But if he is encouraged and helped by his teacher to read that French book, viewed in the light of *communication*, he will soon get all the information out of that book that he requires.

Take a more striking example. Business or pleasure takes us to—let us say—Germany, and we do not know German. That pedant of a schoolmaster who is of our party starts swotting at German as a *code*. And while he is entangled in the mysteries of the declension and conjugation the more practical of us soon discover that *Wieviel? Wo? Geben Sie, Ich will*, and a few dozen such expressions helped out with gestures, enable us to express three-quarters of our needs.

Yet another example—this time from the classroom.

'Come here quickly', says the teacher.

STUDENT. Come here quick.

TEACHER. Come here quick*ly*. [*Three seconds gone, in which the student might have learned 'tomorrow' or 'lavatory' or any other useful expression of an idea that he might want to communicate.*]

Again, the teacher asks, 'What do you say when you want somebody to shut the door?'

The student answers, 'If I will that anyone close door I will tell to him, "Be so good to close door".'

The correction of this answer takes up ten whole minutes, during which time the student might have been taught how to communicate twenty useful ideas

And so on *ad infinitum*.

In a word, the teacher is wasting the students' time by his cult of accuracy—he is diminishing his students' possibilities that he is desired, and paid, to *increase*.

If I had my way every prospective teacher or professor of English or French or German—or whatever the language may be—would be compelled, as part of his training, to live for a year in some foreign country of which the language is unknown to him, and where his language is unknown to those constituting his sole environment, with a bilingual dictionary as his single textbook or guide-book. At the end of that period he would be bound to realize what a language is, and what it is not. He would come to realize as he could not otherwise realize, that a language in its essence is nothing other than a mode of communication.

Comments on Letter 4
We had considered that 'as a code' and 'as communication' came to the same thing. However, by comparing the two letters supporting these theories, we see that the respective conceptions may be entirely distinct and contradictory. The code people postulate *accuracy*, the communication people disregard it.

The writer of Letter 4, however, scoffing at codes as he does, is proposing a code himself, a code that consists of a collection of first-aid expressions for the use of the tourist and traveller—in fact, any person who is using the language for subordinate purposes.

LETTER 5. THE LANGUAGE AS SOUNDS
You ask me what essentially is that thing called English or French, etc., as the case may be—in short 'a language'. Had you not stressed the word 'essentially' I might have answered that a language is a series of intelligible symbols by means of which we express or communicate thoughts, ideas, notions, and concepts. But in its essence, regarded purely objectively, shorn of all its accretions and special attributes, a language is nothing other than (on the part of the speaker) a succession of articulations, or (on the part of the hearer) a succession of sounds, which, in the course of development of the language, have become associated with meanings. (For the sake of conciseness, and to avoid the cumbrous repetition of the term 'articulations or sounds' I will shorten it to 'sounds', it being understood that I mean 'articulations or sounds'.)

Those who have given little or no thought to the subject may have the idea that a language consists in its essence of letters and written words; those who are addicted to literolatry go farther and maintain as a pious conviction the thesis that a language that has no written form (and hence no literature) is not a language at all, but a jargon. These letter-worshippers see in a language nothing but the letters with which it is conventionally written. They associate language with literature to such an extent that for them 'language' is synonymous with 'literature'. The person who is more than usually proficient in the use of a language they call 'a man of *letters*', otherwise a *littérateur*; and one who uses his language in accordance with what Sapir calls the 'drift' of that language, who uses it spontaneously and naturally, instead of using it in accordance with the arbitrary rules imposed on him by pedants and grammarians—such a one is termed *illiterate*, or, at best, *unlettered*. Fowler,[1] for one, pillories 'Instead of me being dismissed' as an *illiteracy*. All of which shows that in the minds of those who would transform the science of linguistics into a cult, with the classic authors as its gods, with the dictionary and grammar as its holy books, and with the grammarians as its high-priests, a language is nothing but letters. Their reaction towards language is emotional. These survivors of medievalism interpret language solely in the light of that medieval ignorance that was disguised as enlightenment. For in matters linguistic the scholars of the Renaissance period, blinded by their adoration of the written word—preferably written in Latin or Greek—fought ignorance with ignorance, and founded the tradition that the *lingua* was as naught and the *litera* as all. Their modern descendants run true to type and maintain this tradition. 'You would study a foreign language,' they say. 'Here, take this *book*. Begin at the beginning and study the *alphabet* of the language. Begin at the ABC.' And thus those that they so ill advise plunge themselves into the study not of the language, but of that accessory that is the conventional— and often artificial—writing system associated with that language.

For about writing systems (as about religions) have grown a glamour, a mysterious charm, a sentimental and emotional appeal—something that would merit our sympathetic admiration were it confined to legitimate channels, and not foisted on a scientific world as if this glamour were a series of proven truths. It is not for nothing that the very word 'glamour' is cognate with the word 'grammar', and that the 'spells' cast by the necromancer have their modern counterpart in the 'spellings' of the orthographists. The poet and priest have their functions, but when they impose their subjective notions on those who are out to secure objective truths they become positive dangers to the advancement of learning.

And so, according to these obscurantists, the written word is the real word, the archetype; and the spoken word is its ephemeral—and distorted—reflection.

---

[1] In his *Modern English Usage*. Clarendon Press, 1926.

Nor is the tradition confined to the West. You would learn Arabic or Urdu? The *munshi* or the pundit who is to guide you comes and presents you with the alphabet of the language. You would learn Chinese or Japanese? The Oriental teacher promptly produces his book in which are inscribed, not the sounds of the Chinese or Japanese languages, but the ideographs with which those languages have the misfortune to be written.

Now this is wrong; it is all topsy-turvy, and the wonder is that these medievalists, these pedants, these *munshi* and pundits and other obscurantists, have been able to put it over for so long. Utterly mistaken, the victims of their own linguistic illusions, they are still able to find victims in their turn, and to impose on these their fanatical doctrines; and the victims in their turn impose them on others.

The written form of a language is no more part of that language than the Morse Code or Pitman's Shorthand is part of English. So far from the spoken word being a vague, fleeting, and variable reflection of the written word, the exact contrary is the case. The written word is to the spoken word what the photograph of a landscape is to the landscape itself, what the printed page of music is to the music itself, what the picture of a triangle is to the mathematical conception of a triangle.

Professor H. C. Wyld has made the same point in his *Growth of English*:[1]

What is writing? It is simply a clever and convenient device by which certain symbols, which we call *letters*, are used to represent the sounds of speech. Words are built up of a collection of several sounds, and so when we write we are supposed to use a letter for each sound of which the word is composed. Letters in themselves are not language, but merely symbols which are used for the sounds of which language is composed. There is no life or meaning in written symbols by themselves; but they must be translated, as it were, into the sounds for which they stand before they become language or have any meaning. We become so accustomed to the look of letters, in groups to represent words, that we learn to read them off quite rapidly into the sounds for which they stand. Even when we read silently, without pronouncing the words aloud, we carry out the process mentally, and often unconsciously, of turning the letters into the sounds which each represents, and in this way we get at the meaning of what is written.

We have already said that the sounds of speech themselves are only the symbols of thoughts, not the thoughts themselves. Written words, however,

[1] Murray, 1923.

are still farther away from the thoughts and ideas than spoken ones, for they
are only the symbols of these spoken ones—that is to say, they are symbols of
symbols.

Spoken language, then, comes first, and is the reality of speech; written
words are a late invention, and have no life beyond that which the reader puts
into them, when he pronounces the sounds for which they were written.

The literolaters hold up a book to us and say, 'Lo, this is English!'
or point to another book and say, 'Behold, that is French!' Nothing of
the sort! Those books contain printed words which, bereft of the
delicate shades of sounds with their assimilations, weakenings, tones,
stresses, and prominences, are but poor fogged photographs of the
crisp living originals.

The acoustics engineer holding before us his strips of oscillograms,
or his magnified sections of the groove of a gramophone record, has a
better right to point to these things and to call them English or French,
for these are at least true photographs reproducing everything that was
in the original—except life. For these, by means of engineering
devices, may be made to reproduce the originals as they were originally
spoken.

For fifty thousand years, for a hundred thousand years, or more
maybe, language has existed. Until writing came to be invented some
five thousand years ago—and rude picture-writing at that—it was
impossible that a language could appear to be other than its reality—
a succession of sounds; and even today the vast majority of languages
are unwritten. As in the history of the language, so in the history of
the individual language-user. Until he learns to read and write (and
the great majority of language-users have learned to do neither) he
knows his language only in its pure essence—as successions of sounds
that have usually become more or less associated with meanings.

I say advisedly that a language in its essence is not a succession of
spoken words—for words are but arbitrary divisions of language.
Were it not for such arbitrary divisions devised by orthographists
English might be written as it is spoken, and figure in printed form
insuchwiseasthis, forafterall thereisnohardandfastline tobe drawnbet-
ween onewordandanother. 'Another' looks more natural than the
more logical 'an other,' and English people write as 'cannot' what
many Americans prefer to see as 'can not'; 'nevertheless' would look
odd as 'never the less', and 'notwithstanding' almost unintelligible if
written 'not with standing'.

We hear our language in the form of 'slices of sonority',[1] and each slice, thanks to its context and environment, becomes associated with the idea or ideas that it symbolizes.

If we exclude oscillograms and the magnifications of the grooves of gramophone records phonetic transcription alone can show in written form the slices of sonority of which a language is made up. If we want the most exact photographs of living language that are intelligible in terms of letters it is phonetic transcription that provides them.

The average student of a foreign language complains that the slices of sonority uttered by the native speaker have very little resemblance to the written words which are supposed to represent them. The English student of French hears a Frenchman deliver the slices of sonority which we transcribe here:

> [vulevuvniri'si?]
> [oksɛ'bo!]
> [ʒlɛvytuta'lœːr]

and fails to associate them with:

> Voulez-vous venir ici?
> Oh, que c'est beau!
> Je l'ai vu tout-à-l'heure.

A French student of English hears an Englishman deliver slices of sonority which we transcribe here as:

> [əkwɔːtrəvə'naʊə]
> [eɪ'twiːksəgoʊ]
> [wʌnəðəbɛstɪg'zaːmplzaɪnoʊ]

and fails to associate them with:

> A quarter of an hour.
> Eight weeks ago.
> One of the best examples I know.

Why don't these people pronounce the language as it is written? That is the complaint. And the form in which this complaint is made reveals the fallacy under which the complainers are labouring—the false reasoning which is due to the traditional teachings of the medieval pedant and the Oriental pundit. For the Frenchman and the Englishman do indeed pronounce their languages as they are written by phoneticians, who alone realize that the slices of sonority uttered by

---

[1] See A. Séchehaye and C. Bally, *Cours de linguistique générale*. Payot, 1916.

the native speakers constitute the real language, the language in its
essence; and that orthographies some centuries behind the times—
fantastic orthographies at that—are but caricatures of the real thing.

If you present the language in its true form, a series of slices of
sonority, all becomes clear and intelligible. Present it in its artificialized
form, that of alphabetic convention, arbitrary word-division, grammar
that forces all languages into the narrow moulds of classical tradition—
moulds that were good enough for Latin, but are not nearly good
enough for 'English, French, German, Spanish, etc.'—and, naturally
enough, the language, distorted and cramped beyond measure,
becomes a thing of mystery, a source of perplexity, the despair of the
rationalist, and the Cinderella of the scientist and the artist alike.

Break the bonds imposed on language by the medievalists of the
world's universities (be they in England, Russia, America, or India),
destroy the cult of the letter-worshippers, expose the fallacies and
superstitions of those who prefer the obscurity and mystery of orthographic glamour to the clear, all-searching light of modern phonetics,
and you will deliver language from the blight that has for all too long
paralysed its study, and will show language as it really is.

Comments on Letter 5
We applaud much that our correspondent says—but he protests too
much. He would set up one fetish—slices of sonority—for another—
slices of orthography. Not all concepts are couched in terms of sonority;
some have become enshrined in terms of orthography. The ideas
of semantics, phonetics, orthology (in fact, most of the ideas connected
with modern linguistics), have first taken their form as spellings (with
their articulated equivalents subsidiary). All linguisticians know what
the word 'sandhi' means, but not all are prepared to articulate the word.
Even the ingenious words 'literolatry' and 'literolatist' flow more freely
from the pen than from the tongue. Fortunately the writer has abstained
from the use of the word 'speech', for we feared that he would
describe his attitude with the term 'speech'—which would prejudice
the case of those who use this term with a different connotation.

LETTER 6. THE LANGUAGE AS SPEECH
You ask me what is a language in its essence—that is to say, a language
stripped of all fortuitous or subsidiary attributes and accretions. If you
will permit me I should like to answer you out of my personal history
as a thinker about languages and their ways.

Ten years ago I should have answered your question in this way: 'Language is communication, particularly oral communication, together with the code that systematizes that communication.' It seemed to me at the time that this was the broadest and most exact interpretation of the term 'language'. To communicate is to speak or write; in order to speak or write we must have words and a knowledge of their conventional values, arrangement, and manipulation. Language, then, is the thing you communicate with and how to use it. Or, as Sapir[1] puts it: 'Language is a purely human and non-instinctive method of communicating ideas, emotions, and desires by means of a system of voluntarily produced symbols.'

It was on these grounds, then, and solely on these grounds, that I advocated and practised the use of such teaching methods as would give the pupil adequate opportunities for communicating in the foreign language, and relating all his linguistic experience to communication. For example, I advocated and practised oral direct-method procedures. I called out *'Levez-vous'*, and the pupils stood up. Accompanying the instructions by the necessary gestures and movements, I said, *'Voici un livre'*, or *'Le livre est sur la table'*, or *'Je vais à la porte'*. I then asked such questions as *'Qu'est-ce que c'est?'* *'Qu'est-ce que je fais?'* and looked as if I wanted to know. When I called the roll I got the answer *'Présent!'* in the language I was teaching. The pupils at that moment were conscious of giving me a vital piece of information concerning themselves—that is to say, they were using language for what I then believed to be its essential purpose, communication. But I didn't teach them that *Levez-vous* is French for 'Stand up' or that *présent* is French for 'present', because if I had they would have taken these things in the same way as they took such pieces of instruction as 'William the Conqueror, 1066', something to be known and stored, rather than something to be used in the form of acts of communication.

I also advocated and employed such other methods as would enable the pupils to use effectively the highly complicated code which I believed a language, as viewed by a foreigner, to be. For example, when, by a process of communications, I had familiarized the pupils with the fact that the future endings of *parler*, *donner*, and *demander* are -*erai*, -*eras*, -*era*, and so on, I told them, just like the old-fashioned grammarians that all the other -*er* verbs behave in the same way. In short, I used a 'code' technique. I flatter myself that I did it better

---

[1] In his *Language, an Introduction to the Study of Speech*. Harcourt, Brace, 1921.

than most people, because I was very careful in making my classifications to classify the existing language as used in ordinary communication, and not its philological or historical excrescences.

I say I should have answered you in this way because I had to give an answer, but it would have been with a great deal of mental reservation and some uncertainty. If a language were essentially communication it would be serving its proper function only when used for communicating, but we are fully aware that such is not the case. For example, the process called 'thinking aloud' in privacy cannot by any reasonable stretch of definition be called 'communication', but it is certainly 'use of language'. Going further and supposing that the thinking is not done aloud, that no sounds are actually produced, and even that there is no movement of the articulatory organs, nevertheless language is being used in the process. The form which our thoughts take is a linguistic one, and therefore it is surely legitimate to say that language is being used in an activity that one could hardly describe as communication. Still another example: I remember that when I had been living in France for some years I was suddenly surprised to find myself conscious one day that I had been dreaming the previous night in French. Because of its unfamiliarity I was conscious of having dreamed in French, but the natural corollary of this realization was that all my previous dreaming activity had been conducted in my native language.

I was not only dissatisfied with my communication definition; my conception of a language as a code, also, did not seem to fit the facts entirely. My first cause of dissatisfaction was the fact that I could not hide from myself that my attitude towards language had been influenced by teaching a language as a foreign language. The conditions under which a foreign language has to be taught differ widely from those under which a native language is acquired, but the principal difference is in the immeasurably shorter time that can be devoted to the process. This being the case, the teacher of the foreign language is perpetually in search of short cuts; and the organization of short cuts is codification. 'Here is a mass of phenomena; let's sort it out so that it may be acquired, if not more effectively, at any rate more quickly.' I, as this teacher of a foreign language, found that to a certain extent I could sort out the phenomena that I had to inculcate—in short, I discovered that a language was codifiable. But to say that something is codifiable is not to prove that it is essentially a code. Law is an excellent example of something that is codifiable—so codifiable, indeed, that in most countries of the world it *is* codified. But we are well aware that law in its essence is organized custom prompted by primitive superstitions and taboos, and repeated tryings out of the mass-consciousness of what constitutes equity. In simpler terms, law is a growth of custom later made for convenience into a code. Similarly languages, resulting from a long historical development, guided and directed by the mass-consciousness of what constitutes adequate expression, have been made later for convenience into codes. Moreover, I, in company with all my compatriots, am conscious of the fact that my own language is not a code to me; I happen to know that it is codified in the so-called grammars for English students and in the much more scientific (though much less historical) grammars for foreign students. But I possess my language certainly not because of—probably in spite of— either of these codifications.

If, then, language is communication, but something more than communication; if it is codifiable, but not essentially a code, what is it? What is that quality of language which makes it a fitting means of communication, which renders it codifiable and yet transcends both these definitions? I have come to the conclusion that a language, considered fundamentally and shorn of its accidentals and by-products, is nothing other than, and nothing less than, *the thing that we think with: the instrument of thought.*

It is often said that words are the mere garment of thought, and within certain limitations this is unquestionably true. That thought preceded language is not only the considered opinion of an authority on the subject like Sapir but must be the natural conclusion of any intelligent layman. Watch a baby and see how it struggles with an evident desire to define a need or a perception: thought is going on, and, side by side with the process of thought, sounds are made, usually the familiar *goo-goo-goo.* Articulate the word 'milk' several times and watch the intense satisfaction on the child's face as he handles—or rather mouths—that first thought-instrument. 'Milk', he says, and 'Milk' again, and ever afterwards identifies that puzzling, indefinable thought with the new instrument that you have given him. His thought has been crystallized because it has been given an instrument or a garment, or what you will. And from that day onward it is a clearer thought because of the garment you have provided to give it shape.

I wonder if you remember that striking story by H. G. Wells entitled *The Invisible Man?* By a certain process the man in question made his actual body entirely invisible. When from time to time he

wished to take his normal place in the world he would put on a suit
of clothes, boots, gloves, face-bandages, and a hat, and by this process
became a visible man. Language, clothing thought in the same way,
makes it visible to others by communication, but no less does it make
it visible to the thinker. The invisible man, once clothed, could see his
own shape; in the same way the shape of a thought can be perceived
only when clothed in language.

Sapir[1] puts the same point in this way:

Most people, asked if they can think without speech, would probably answer,
'Yes, but it is not easy for me to do so. Still I know it can be done.' Language
is but a garment! But what if language is not so much a garment as a prepared
road or groove? It is, indeed, in the highest degree likely that language is an
instrument originally put to uses lower than the conceptual plane and that
thought arises as a refined interpretation of its content. The product grows,
in other words, with the instrument, and thought may be no more conceivable,
in its genesis and daily practice, without speech than is mathematical reasoning practicable without the lever of an appropriate mathematical symbolism.
No one believes that even the most difficult mathematical proposition is
inherently dependent on an arbitrary set of symbols, but it is impossible to
suppose that the human mind is capable of arriving at or holding such a
proposition without the symbolism. The writer, for one, is strongly of the
opinion that the feeling entertained by so many that they can think, or even
reason, without language is an illusion. The illusion seems to be due to a number of factors. The simplest of these is the failure to distinguish between
imagery and thought.[2] As a matter of fact, no sooner do we try to put an
image into conscious relation with another than we find ourselves slipping
into a silent flow of words. Thought may be a natural domain apart from the
artificial one of speech, but speech would seem to be the only road we know
of that leads to it.

Now what are the practical applications of this general thesis so ably
expressed by Sapir and by this time almost universally maintained by
psychologists and linguisticians? If language is the thing we think with
it is only fulfilling its proper function when it is used for thinking.
Our success as speakers and users of our own tongue is due entirely to

[1] *Op. cit.*

[2] Sapir's distinction between imagery and thought is surely exemplified by the work
of the 'stream of consciousness' novelists. They definitely reject thought, and confine
themselves to a reproduction of the images to which Sapir refers.

our capacity for, and experience in, thinking with it. The more we think with our own language, the better we know it, and this simple truism should surely apply to our experience with a foreign language. The process of thinking with a language is the process of conscious or unconscious articulation. What we have to do, then, as learners of a foreign language is to develop a capacity to employ that process of conscious or unconscious articulation of the symbolic sounds which that language contains. We have to develop in the foreign language that sound-sense which we possess in our own. As Palmer has pointed out,[1] 'We test [language] forms by articulating them . . . We are unable to judge the correctness or incorrectness of a construction in our own language until we have submitted it to the articulation test.' That is the point. To possess an articulation standard in the foreign language is to possess that language in the *way*, if not in the *measure*, that the native possesses it. To know that *Je ne vous en ai pas donné* is good French, not because it obeys all the so-called rules for the position of negative particles, personal pronouns, and auxiliary and principal verbs, but simply because it *sounds* right, is to know French not necessarily as well as a Frenchman, but at least like a Frenchman. Is the French word *silence* masculine or feminine? On what ground does the Frenchman decide? He decides on no ground at all, but simply on the sound of it. To substitute *sound* for *ground* as a reason for correctness: that should be the aim of the language-learner as it is the regular practice of the native language-knower. Let there be no mistake. This is not something that applies only to the spoken language; we try out our written sentences in the same way. It is sound, and not ground, which guides the pen, just as it guides the tongue. A good written style in one's own language, or in a foreign one, is simply a collection of those words and constructions which, when combined in a certain order, sound right on paper.

Now what is the difference between the knowledge of English of my seventy-year-old German friend, Professor Schmidt, and that of my seven-year-old son? The professor knows, at a moderate estimate, ten times as many words as his junior competitor and, estimating with equal moderation, three times as many grammar mechanisms. And yet, in some subtle way, my son knows English 'better' than the professor. What is that quality of 'better' which we all recognize, but rarely trouble to define? The average person will answer, 'Your son

---

[1] *The Oral Method of Teaching Languages.* Heffer, 1921, p. 22.

knows it like a native, and the professor like a foreigner.' What does this mean? In precise terms, it means that my son is using English as an instrument of thought and as an instrument of extending thought, an instrument of effort towards new thought, whereas the professor is using it as a collection of symbols for other thought which is being carried on with another instrument—viz. his mother-tongue. The same average layman will comment on this statement something in this wise: 'Yes, I agree with you, but that is a difference which is inherent in the situation.' It isn't.

I have two other friends, both in their thirties, both Frenchmen. One of them, Pierre, has an English vocabulary twice as large as that of the other, Jacques, and also possesses half as many grammar-mechanisms again as the other. Pierre's English (written or spoken) is like Professor Schmidt's English; Jacques' English isn't. To the superficial hearer or reader it is simply 'better' than Pierre's, and again the 'better' means that he is using English when dealing with English—as an instrument of thought. Now Jacques doesn't speak English as I do (nor does my son, by the way), but he uses English in the same way—though not in the same quantity—as he uses French. Jacques, then, has reached at thirty a linguistic position that my son has reached at seven. *That* discrepancy *is* inherent in the situation, but it is the *only* one. The point that I wish to make by all this is that, as language is essentially an instrument of thought, it is only when the learner is using it as an instrument of thought that he is on the road to that real proficiency in it which the layman describes vaguely as 'good'. Also, I want to point out that this has nothing to do with the *quantity* of language acquired; but with the *attitude* towards what has been acquired and what will be acquired in the future.

Casting round in my mind for a convenient expression to replace the cumbrous 'as the instrument of thought', I have decided upon 'as speech'. I have decided on this term, not because it is ideally suitable, not because I imagine that the term is self-explanatory, and by its very nature suggests what I wish it to imply, but because I can hit on no other term nearly so appropriate. I am aware that I am using the term 'speech' in a new and special sense, and that by so doing I am running the risk that you who read my letter will jump to the conclusion that I am advocating the claims of the oral method of teaching languages to the exclusion of all other methods, or that the spoken form of the language is more important than the written. I am not talking about 'spoken English' or 'English as speaking'. If an unambiguous term existed that would concretize the conception of language that I have outlined in the present letter I should certainly use that term. I could, it is true, coin a new term—one perfectly unambiguous—to serve as a distinctive label for this conception, but a specially coined term is frequently incomprehensible—additional evidence, incidentally, of the fact that the majority of people think only in terms of familiar language. The term 'speech' is already used by psychologists, phoneticians, teachers of the deaf and dumb, logicians, and others, with so many different connotations that an additional one will not be too great a violation of accepted usage. In selecting this term to serve as a label for my conception of the essence of language I am influenced by the fact that the word 'speech' is more or less equivalent to the French word *parole*, which has been used by de Saussure and his followers to designate the same (or a very similar) conception.

I understand that the contents of this letter are intended to guide you in the choice of heads of the various language departments in your institute. I would therefore suggest that you secure the services of a person who is convinced that the attitude which one must have towards a language is essentially the one that I have outlined. He can be deeply versed in the national literature or in philological lore, or he can be ignorant of these. But he should accept the truth of this funda- mental conception of a language as speech, and be prepared to subordinate all his teaching to the attainment of that attitude in his students.

P.S. By the way, I have dilated at such length on my new discoveries that I may perhaps have given you the impression that I would now teach language by methods other than those I used ten years ago. I wouldn't. I'd use the same methods, but for better reasons. All these methods—direct method, oral method, natural method, and the rest— I see now were but gropings towards the 'as speech' attitude. May I add another little word, which may surprise you? Now that I'm so sure of the right attitude I'm less worried about methods. Once I'm sure that my students possess whatever little bit of French, German, etc., they may happen to have 'as speech', I'm quite prepared to let them do a little translation or even to talk to them about grammar if they like. The only trouble with grammar and translation methods is that in the early stages they militate against the 'as speech' attitude, and the chief merit of direct-oral-natural method procedures is that they foster the 'as speech' attitude.

Comments on Letter 6

This letter seems to contain the most unassailable conception of a language. What the writer has said is summed up in his expression 'language is the thing you think with'. Now we are perfectly well aware that there are a number of persons who have examined this categorical thesis and have found it wanting. Even Sapir, whom our correspondent quotes with greater ingenuity than honesty, shows quite clearly that thought is possible without language, and Jespersen points out, with many examples, that language is put to a number of uses that have nothing to do with thought as it is usually understood.[1] Nevertheless, in spite of the facts that a good deal of thinking is done without language and that a good deal of language is used without thought, we feel, with our correspondent, that it is fair to say that in these days, when almost all mankind is possessed of a language of some kind or other, most of the thought in the world is done by means of language, and, on the other hand, most of the language used is used for the purpose of expressing thought. If we accept our correspondent's statement with the modifications stated above, it is obvious that a language is only fulfilling its proper function when it is being thought with. This idea can be taken as a basis for every language course in the Institute from Lesson 1, where we force the student to think *book* when he says 'Book', to Lesson 101, when, without any forcing at all, he thinks with the language of Meredith when he is reading Meredith. That, as it appears to us, is the great merit of this conception—that it has something to say, some guidance to give, on every course that we may be called upon to provide. It is comprehensive because it is more than a method; it is an attitude. We feel that there is no possible aspect of what is called English, French, German, Spanish, etc., in the teaching of which this fundamental principle can find no place.

We hear much of the 'natural method'; as a matter of fact, the natural method is a hundred methods, or even no method at all. The secret of the native child's success in acquiring his language is not in the method, which, as we say, is variegated, and sometimes non-existent; it is in the attitude which the native child has towards his language—an attitude imposed on him by circumstances. The writer of this letter is not the exponent of a natural method; he insists merely on the attainment of a natural attitude. The adult balks at learning a language in the same *way* as a child does, but the writer is merely

[1] In his chapter on 'Speech and Language', in *Mankind, Nation, and Individual from a Linguistic Point of View*, Williams and Norgate, 1925.

asking him to learn in the same *spirit* as does the child. If he will not learn in that spirit he will never come to feel that language, for you cannot learn a spirit—you can only learn to feel a spirit—and whether our students want to know the language in order to write invoices or read Proust, this attitude is an essential prerequisite.

2 Learning

H. V. R. Well, we've seen what these 'producers' of language as a
teachable commodity have to say, and we've made up our minds that
the writer of Letter 6 has got nearest to the essential English, French,
or whatever it is. But even when we were answering the others so
categorically we felt that there was a lot in what they had to say.
Still, we do feel that No. 6 cuts right through them, and it seems
to me what we've got to do now is to see how, taking the No. 6 idea
as the essential, we have to modify it to meet the specific needs of the
consumers.

H. E. P. Yes. From the experience I have had in connexion with
foreign language institutes and private pupils, the chief difficulty is
the consumer. No matter what method you have adopted, there will
always be some 50 per cent of the learners who object to that particular
method. You adopt the direct method—a certain number of students
don't like the direct method discipline; they want every word and
construction-pattern explained in terms of their own language. In
another case and place it is some form of translation method you have
adopted—a certain number of pupils want the direct method only.
Or you provide phonetics, and the pupils won't have it. Or you refuse
to provide phonetics, and a certain number of students send in their
resignations because it's phonetics they want.

H. V. R. Of course, we know of the captiousness of students, but it's
not so much a question of giving them what they want as of giving
them what they'll stand, so that they will learn more effectively.
There's no disputing the fact that if we have to overcome resistances all
the time progress is going to be slow with the best method in the world.
Besides, it *is* conceivable that a method could be adopted to suit special
needs without any sacrifice of the *principles* of the method.

H. E. P. I doubt whether a method based on a doctrine can ever be adapted to suit special needs. Here we have a Henry Sweet who maintains that all approaches to language must be on a strictly phonetic basis, who will not allow learners so much as to see the orthographic forms of words until they have spent a year on phonetic transcription. Or you have a Berlitz who cannot yield 1 per cent from his attitude towards the 100 per cent direct method; who in yielding 1 per cent would be prejudicing fatally the cardinal principle for which he stands.

H. V. R. I think you misunderstand me a little. And I think the best way of considering the whole situation is on the analogy of medicine. The doctor asks the patient what's wrong with him—in other words, what he wants to be right with him. I assert, then, that we should ask our prospective pupils what they want to be right with them—that is, in other words, what they want to do with the English and French they learn.

H. E. P. And then you prescribe?

H. V. R. No, we don't prescribe just yet. A medical man doesn't prescribe a treatment for the disease that the patient thinks he's suffering from; he listens to the patient's description of his abnormal sensations; he listens to the patient's deductions from these sensations, for what they're worth, and then he proceeds to diagnose, with a view to prescription.

H. E. P. Does the parallel hold good? What do you mean, in the actual case of a prospective language-student, by the patient who 'describes his abnormal sensations' and the doctor 'who proceeds to diagnose'?

H. V. R. The parallel is pretty exact. Your student comes along and complains, for instance, that, whereas he reads the foreign language with facility, he is unable to converse in that language. His deduction is that he needs what he calls 'conversation lessons'. We listen to the exposition of his case and his deduction. We have reason, however, to doubt the validity of his deduction, and, like the doctor, proceed to an objective diagnosis of the case, also with a view to prescription. The result of the diagnosis shows conclusively, to our technical perceptions, that it is not merely incapacity to converse which is his trouble. His trouble is due to a number of contributory causes, the sum of which makes it impossible for him, among other things, to carry on a conversation in the foreign language.

H. E. P. Yes, your parallel's all right. We proceed to the diagnosis;

we come to know with fair exactness what is the thing that our prospective student not only feels himself subjectively to be lacking, but
what, as a matter of fact, he actually is lacking. And then we shall set
about the prescribing.

H. V. R. What you mean is that we shall indicate to him first what it
is that he really needs, and then the best means of acquiring it.

H. E. P. Yes, and on the two counts we are going to meet with resistances. The student will dispute first our diagnosis of his needs, and
secondly our prescription. That's where your parallel does break down,
after all; for the patient, however much he may object to and resist
the treatment, will never dispute the findings of the diagnosis.

H. V. R. Won't he, by Jove! I've spent a good part of my life in
hospitals, and the one topic of conversation is disputing the diagnosis
of the doctors, when, of course, as you say, the patients aren't arguing
against or deliberately evading the treatment. But, still, that's beside
the point. There's no doubt that we shall get our twofold resistances.
And I suggest that we're as much within our rights as the doctor in
saying, 'If you won't accept the diagnosis and/or you won't follow the
treatment, get out of our clinic and get another doctor'.

H. E. P. But we can't do that until we've made an attempt at classification of the abnormal sensations of our prospective patients. Medical
science is built up on a study of diseases; cases of disease have been
collected and classified. The doctor's capacity to diagnose and ultimately to prescribe is based on the collection of cases of abnormality
that he has known directly through personal experience, and indirectly
through study. Linguistic science is, alas, not so far developed as
medical science, and we can rely less on reported abnormalities as a
basis for diagnosis. We have to rely mainly on the cases we can observe
ourselves. What we really want is a good collection of cases.

H. V. R. All right, then, let's set about getting them. From these
producer fellows we've worked out what we consider to be the essential
thing we've got to teach. I suggest that from the consumers we get
as many varied statements of needs as possible and then classify them,
and, according to the classification, work out the different kinds of
application of what we consider to be the fundamental method to
meet those needs.

H. E. P. When we were in doubt as to what a language is in its
essence we sent out letters to authorities on English, French, German,
etc.; we received their replies, which were mutually exclusive and
collectively exhaustive statements of opinion, and drew conclusions

from them. Suppose we repeat the process here, and send out letters to prospective students inquiring of them what sort of English (or whatever the foreign language may be) they want to learn, and how they want it taught. When these prospective students have given us their various exclusive-exhaustive points of view—the disciplines that they'll welcome, the disciplines that they'll stand, and the disciplines that they'll resist—we shall know better how to set about catering for the reasonable requirements and ignoring the unreasonable requirements.

H. V. R. Yes, that's perfectly sound from our point of view. The only trouble is that you won't get all these lads telling you how they want language taught in advance. That part of the business will come once you've started teaching them.

H. E. P. Well, we'll hope they'll rationalize. And, in any case, we'll send letters out to headmasters and to parents. *They*'ve got a clear idea of how they want languages taught.

And these were the letters:

(a) *To a Prospective Language Student of Riper Years*

DEAR SIR,

We understand that you wish to take lessons in French [German, Spanish], and we wish to confess to you that although we have spent a great many years in the teaching of French [German, Spanish] and the organization of such teaching, we are still in some doubt as to what ground should be covered in the lessons we organize. We are therefore asking you as a prospective student of our institute to ask yourself, and to tell us, what you really mean when you say you want to learn French [German, Spanish]—in other words, what sort of French [German, Spanish] you wish to learn. We venture to add for your guidance that your answer will be in a measure dictated by your age and circumstances, and by the uses to which you wish to put your knowledge of French [German, Spanish] when you have acquired it.

Moreover, we wish to put another question, which may seem to you somewhat strange. Having decided upon a full answer to the first question, you are asked to tell us how you would have us teach you the French [German, Spanish] you wish to learn, and particularly to which of the linguistic disciplines known to you you would be willing to submit yourself. We put this second question because, whatever else in this whole language-learning business we are uncertain about, we are at least convinced that ultimate success depends upon an absence of conscious or subconscious resistance on the part of the student to the methods employed, and we wish as far as possible to approximate our methods to your needs and also to your known capacities.

3

(*b*) *To the Headmaster (or Principal) of a Secondary (or High) School who proposes to place his Language Courses in the Hands of Outside Experts*

DEAR SIR,

We very much appreciate the honour you have paid us in proposing to place your pupils in our charge for purposes of language-study. Your proposal indicates that you feel that language-study is of sufficient importance to justify entrusting it to specialists. But we fully realize that we cannot give this language instruction without any regard to the general curriculum of your school. It is manifestly your duty as a headmaster to correlate all the subjects which your students are taught in such a way as to ensure that they receive a balanced education.

We are therefore requesting you to state as fully as possible (1) what sort of French [German, Spanish] you wish your students to learn (giving as far as possible your reasons), and (2) how you wish this French [German, Spanish] to be taught, with particular reference to disciplines, either purely linguistic or generally psychological. We feel in conscience bound to state that we cannot guarantee to incorporate all your suggestions in our course of study, but we can assure you that we shall make every effort to do so commensurate with the effective fulfilment of our side of the bargain—viz. the provision of scientific language instruction.

(*c*) *To a Parent who desires his Child, of Secondary School Age, to learn a Language*

DEAR SIR OR MADAM,

We shall be very pleased to receive ———— as a pupil of the institute. The grading here will depend not only on ————'s present knowledge of French [German, Spanish], but also on your wishes with regard to what we are calling the 'kind' of French [German, Spanish] you wish ———— to learn. You will appreciate that the term 'French' ['German', 'Spanish'] is susceptible of a number of interpretations, and in the instruction of ———— we wish as far as possible to be governed by your interpretation. We should therefore be obliged if you would state the ultimate uses to which you wish ———— to put the French [German, Spanish] that he is to learn.

Closely related to this question of the interpretation of the term 'French' ['German', 'Spanish'] is that of the manner in which instruction should be given. As you are aware, there are certain so-called methods or disciplines, such as the direct method discipline, the oral method discipline, etc., and we therefore request you to state to which discipline or disciplines you would be willing to have ———— subjected.

As before, quite a number of answers were received, but among them eleven stand out as being mutually exclusive and collectively exhaustive, the remainder again being combinations and overlappings of these. The following are the eleven letters.

LETTER 1. A RATIONAL BUT ATROCIOUSLY EXPRESSED ATTITUDE

The sole reason for which I wish to learn Spanish is to become proficient in speaking that language and in understanding it when spoken. I shall often have occasion to visit the countries in which Spanish is spoken, and the better I speak and understand Spanish the greater will be my comfort.

I should therefore wish to learn by what is called, I believe, the 'conversational method'—i.e. to learn spoken Spanish by speaking it. According to those who advocate the conversational method, it is quite easy to learn to read and write a language after one has become proficient in conversation. According to these people also, if one approaches the language by the oral method there is no need to make any special study of grammar; one picks up the grammar as one goes along. I am inclined to agree with such views, which to my mind are based on both common sense and science.

Primarily interested in the spoken language as I am, I should not wish you to think that I am interested in phonetics. The people who teach these phonetics seem to be making a difficult subject still more difficult. It seems to me that in the natural method that I wish to utilize there should be no place for these phonetics, which in their very essence are unnatural. The time one takes in learning phonetics could be more profitably employed in learning how to pronounce the foreign language intelligibly, for I do indeed wish to become fairly proficient in the accent. It is of course, chiefly accent that distinguishes one language from another. Apart from a few outstanding cases, such as the Spanish final *d* or the *z* of *lápiz*, or perhaps the Welsh *ll*, or the peculiar *ng* sound of the French *n* after vowels, or the guttural *ch* of German, sounds do not differ much from language to language; it is this vague quality of *accent* that makes it so difficult to understand the foreigner or to be understood by him.

I repeat, then, that the method that I should wish to follow is the intuitive method, the natural method by which we have learned to speak our mother-tongue—in short, the Berlitz method. For to my mind it is Berlitz who discovered the secret of the success with which Man Friday came to learn the language of Robinson Crusoe. I would, however, make this reservation. According to the Berlitz method, the teacher makes no use of the mother-tongue of the student. This, I think, is a mistake. I should wish my teacher, when necessary, to explain to me in English the meaning of unfamiliar words and constructions, by a comparison between Spanish and English forms, to smooth over these difficulties that unduly retard progress in the earlier stages.

In short, the discipline that I will submit to without resistance—and, indeed, with positive enthusiasm—is that which is associated with the conversational, oral, direct, intuitive, and natural methods.

Comments on Letter 1

We have reproduced this letter chiefly because it exhibits in a comparatively short space one of the largest collections of linguistic fallacies and self contradictions that has ever come to our notice, and at the same time demonstrates the need for precise terms when we discuss this language-learning business. In a greater degree than most of the other contributors to our symposiums, the writer shows the need that there is for a comprehensive term to designate the right attitude towards a language as a subject of study. He is groping around to determine an attitude, and in doing so, in spite of his categoric assurances, he makes manifest the traps and pitfalls with which we are encompassed when we endeavour to set forth clearly our convictions or our prejudices.

We know what he is driving at; we know what is at the back of his mind. He is in a state of revolt against the conventional attitude towards language and language-learning. He reveals also the fact that in his zeal he confounds the antiquarian with those (for instance, the phoneticians) who resist in the maximum degree the dictates of the antiquarians. And if we expose in their crudity the fallacies that underlie the substance of this contribution, it is less with the desire to pillory its inconsistencies than to demonstrate how a lack of adequate terms may militate against a general thesis.

The writer begins by levelling under the common term 'conversational' two different things—the conversational language and the approach to language through speech. Casting around for a term that shall designate the oral approach to language, he hits on the word 'conversational'. He is unfortunate in his choice. He does not really mean the style that is used in informal and intimate communication; he means communication itself. He wishes to stress the fact that the act of communication is a natural process, and not one at the mercy of grammarians or philologists.

He then proceeds to make use of the terms 'conversational', 'oral', 'direct', and 'natural' methods as if they were synonymous.

According to the dictionary, the term 'conversational' means 'fond of, good at, pertaining to, conversation', and the conversational method should therefore mean 'a method of teaching students to become proficient in carrying on a conversation'. This method should include as one of its main features the memorizing of everyday sentences[1] and the subsequent use of them in effective conversational conditions.

The 'oral method', as the term implies, merely designates teaching by the spoken word. The term 'direct method' designates teaching without translation or the use of the student's mother-tongue. The term 'natural method' can be taken to mean only that method by which we learn our native language—i.e. in natural conditions and not studial or classroom conditions—a method very different from the Berlitz method.

He next shows his complete ignorance of phonetics. He is not the only one who supposes the term 'phonetics' to mean 'phonetic symbols'. He is one of the many who do not realize that phonetics (or rather phonetics applied to the study of foreign languages), far from 'making a difficult subject still more difficult', is precisely a science containing practical and detailed instructions as to what are the supposedly difficult foreign sounds, and how to make them. The writer quotes particularly the Spanish final *d*, the *z* of the Spanish word *lápiz*, the Welsh *ll*, what he calls 'the peculiar *ng* sound of the French *n* after vowels', and what he calls 'the guttural *ch* of German'.

Now it is phonetics that tells us that in Spanish both the final *d* (in Castilian) and the *z* of *lápiz* are simply the *th* of 'thin'. It is phonetics that shows us that the Welsh *ll* is just the 'whispered *l*' of the word 'play'. It is phonetics that demonstrates that 'the French *n* after vowels' is not 'a peculiar *ng* sound', but simply an indication that the preceding vowel is produced with the nasal passage open. Phonetics demonstrates also that the German *ch* is not a guttural, but a collection of sounds varying between the first element of the English word 'he' when whispered and that of the word 'who' when whispered.

The statement that there is a 'vague quality of accent that makes it so difficult to understand the foreigner or to be understood by him' is a linguistic fallacy, admirably dealt with by Sapir,[2] who says:

[1] As, for instance, those given in *Everyday Sentences in Spoken English*, by Palmer and Blandford. Heffer, 1922.

[2] *Op. cit.*

The feeling that the average speaker has of his language is that it is built up, acoustically speaking, of a comparatively small number of distinctive sounds, each of which is rather accurately provided for in the current alphabet by one letter or, in a few cases, by two or more alternative letters. As for the languages of foreigners, he generally feels that, aside from a few striking differences that cannot escape even the uncritical ear, the sounds they use are the same as those he is familiar with, but there is a mysterious 'accent' to these foreign languages, a certain unanalysed phonetic character, apart from the sounds as such, that gives them their air of strangeness. This naïve feeling is largely illusory on both scores.

Our correspondent would, moreover, have the Berlitz method, but deprived of the one feature which makes it effective—viz. the learning of the language *through* the language. It is as if he said, 'Ice-cream is my favourite delicacy—especially when slightly warmed.'

And yet, in spite of the inconsistencies, ignorance, and fallacies in which this contribution abounds, the writer on the whole has common-sense views, and wishes for a common-sense approach to the language. His only trouble is that he does not know how to define that approach, and, like so many others, he gives the wrong reasons for the right thing. It is obvious that he wishes to possess Spanish 'as speech', and therefore to approach it 'as speech', but he wishes to do so with those supplementary aids that methodologists have devised in order to quicken the rate of progress of the more adult learner.

As far as his time and circumstances permit we advise him to follow the whole course as outlined in Part 3 of this book up to the end of Stage 5.

LETTER 2. AN APPROACH TO A GROUP OF LANGUAGES SOLELY FROM THE POINT OF VIEW OF A STUDENT OF GENERAL PHONETICS

I am aware that the reason for which I wish to enrol myself as a student in your institute for your Russian course is quite an exceptional one—so exceptional, indeed, that I can hardly expect that you will be able to cater in any large measure for my particular requirements.

I am a student of general phonetics, a subject in which I intend to specialize. This being so, it is my concern and my business to learn how to hear and to reproduce sounds, to know how those sounds are produced, and to be able to analyse them both organically and acoustically. As I am particularly interested in the phenomena of palatalization and velarization I wish to have a first-hand phonetic knowledge of languages in which these phenomena are known to occur.

Beyond the phonetic aspect of languages, there is no aspect that interests me. Their grammatical structure, history, literature, and all that, are matters that have no concern for me. If, therefore, you should impose on me such disciplines as the direct method or the translation method, if you should require of me an intelligent interest in the language either as a code, as a means of communication, as an instrument of thought, or as a spelling system based on a strange and inadequate alphabet, I shall probably resist in a certain measure. I am going to ask you to look upon me more or less as a 'free student', gathering from your courses what is of value to me, and begging to be excused from learning things that are valueless to me. But, on the other hand, I shall be dissatisfied if your teachers withhold from me the data that I am requiring; I shall be dissatisfied if your teachers give me insufficient opportunities for hearing the sounds of the languages that they profess to teach. I shall require of them the utmost severity in their criticisms of my efforts to reproduce the sounds that they are teaching me. I shall from time to time deliberately mispronounce certain sounds, and if the teachers pass my mispronunciations, assuring me that they are all right or good enough, I shall be forced to seek more conscientious teachers.

Your letter invites frankness; had it not done so I should not have been so outspoken in my response.

Comments on Letter 2

We note that our correspondent is not in any general sense a student of language; he is a student of the science of phonetics, a science worthy enough in itself, but one which happens to be merely an auxiliary to the teaching of languages. As, however, it is an important auxiliary, and as we contend that language students must study it at the beginning of their linguistic career, we can cater for our correspondent simply with the ordinary phonetics course which we provide for language students. He will enter the preliminary phonetics classes of any of the languages in which he is interested. What concerns the general theory of phonetics, being familiar ground to him, will not be of value; but to cover that period we shall provide him with a copy of the current number of *Le Maître Phonétique,* and ask him to sit up and take notice when instruction is being given on the specific sounds of the language. Incidentally, he will find the classes for oral assimilation valuable, although he will be using them for purposes other than those of the ordinary students. Finally, we shall recommend him to visit from time to time one or other of the courses listed in Stage 6, where the foreign language is being spoken by the teacher fluently and naturally.

LETTER 3. FROM A STUDENT WHO REQUIRES A SPECIALIST'S VOCABULARY

I admire the frankness with which you have asked me to state my aims in learning Italian and the means which I am prepared to employ under your guidance for the attainment of those aims. I will endeavour to express myself with a similar frankness in order that we may both know where we are and whither we are going. I wish to be able to keep abreast of Italian thought and research in my subject—economics. That is to say, I wish to be able to read, with some measure of under-standing, certain economic reviews and a few of the most important books which appear from time to time on my subject. That's the only purpose for which I wish to learn Italian, and that, consequently, is the only kind of Italian I want to know. I have heard from time to time of commercial Italian, of literary Italian, and of conversational Italian; I have not heard up till now of economic Italian, but if the others exist I see no reason why this one shouldn't. To put it bluntly, then, I am asking you to teach me economic Italian.

How are you going to do it? The answer seems fairly obvious. Your teachers will read with me and others like me some of the books that I have in mind. You will perhaps protest that as I have no elementary knowledge of Italian it will be impossible to commence the study of such difficult texts. To this I would answer (*a*) I know English and French almost equally well, and I have a good grounding in Latin— that is to say, I have experience of the ways of language generally, and I possess most of the elements of any vocabulary which Italian could conceivably contain; (*b*) I am acquainted with the subjects treated in all the publications I wish to read.

It therefore seems to me reasonable to suppose that with the guidance

LEARNING 63

of a competent teacher I can begin from the very first to worry out the meanings of the texts I wish to read, and it is experience in that sort of worrying out which I wish to get. I want to learn the usual turns of expression employed by writers on economics so that I can come to recognize them when I read them. I want to familiarize myself with the Italian equivalents for certain economic terms, not only words (which, after all, I can get from a dictionary), but also such phrases as 'supply and demand', 'value in use', 'unearned increment', 'index number', 'real wages', etc., and I feel that I cannot do better for my purpose than read, with the aid of a teacher able to furnish me with good technical translations when necessary, the texts in which such phrases are sure to occur. As long as I am given that sort of work I shall be perfectly content, for I shall feel: (*a*) that I am doing, right from the beginning, a little of the reading that I want to do—that is to say, that my Italian lessons will serve to give me a part (a small part, of course) of the economic knowledge which I want to get; and (*b*) that I shall be gradually familiarizing myself with the sort of texts that I have to read.

You will complain probably that I shall be getting a very poor knowledge of Italian, and your teacher will want to pause in our reading, either to give me grammatical classifications, saying that the past of the Italian verb is formed in such a way and the present in such another way, or to correct my pronunciation—possibly by a reference to phonetics (of which I know nothing and wish to know nothing)—or to explain Italian syntax, with examples in the vocabulary of another subject. If he does these things he will be wasting his time and mine; and I shall resist. In the course of our reading I shall find out myself the sort of grammatical difficulties which are holding me up; I shall put him questions on those points, and I shall wish for answers concerning those points and concerning no other points. I feel sure that if the procedures that I have outlined are followed I shall succeed in being able to do the one thing I wish to do—viz. read Italian books on economics. I certainly shall not be able to speak Italian, understand spoken Italian, write Italian, or even read Italian, in any general sense. But then, I don't want to, having many other things to do which are for me far more important. You may think that what I am asking of you is something too special but it is my experience that there are numbers of students of various subjects who require just the kind of knowledge of a language that I have described and who would wish to come by it in the way I have outlined.

Comments on Letter 3

We fully realize the legitimacy of our correspondent's aim. He wishes to know just the Italian that is necessary for his particular purpose and no more. The question as to whether he will or will not know *Italian* is, as he rightly says, irrelevant. When he comes to the question of method, however, we cannot refrain from feeling a certain surprise that one who has received an academic training in an exact science should advocate methods which he describes himself as 'worrying out', but which might be more exactly described as 'muddling through'.

Now we do not deny that in the particular circumstances he might muddle through—and muddle through tolerably successfully. He knows French and Latin, languages closely related to Italian—which would make it possible for him to get the acquaintance with Italian he requires or something approximate, even without taking lessons at all. In the peculiar circumstances he would, as we say, muddle through. But we feel that he would continue to muddle through just as long as he had any dealings with the language. If our correspondent has learned French so successfully that he knows that language almost as well as English, his mother-tongue, it is fairly certain that he did not acquire French by the 'muddle-through' process. He must have acquired it by some method more economical than the one that he now proposes, some more organized method enabling him to make a clean job of it. His experience with French must have shown him that organized progress in the language increased not only his knowledge of the language, but also his capacity to acquire further knowledge. By learning more he did more than just learn more; he learned how to learn more. By the disorganized process that he now proposes he may be constantly adding to his knowledge, but none of that knowledge will help him to gain any more; his progress, instead of being 'geometrical', will be merely 'arithmetrical'.

We might add that we do not think that even his self-imposed methods of muddling through will be in any great degree accelerated by his refusal to consider any explanation which his teacher, in full knowledge of the peculiarities of Italian, might feel it desirable to give.

In spite of all this, we say again that, in view of the close relation between the French he knows and the Italian he wishes to know, *tant bien que mal*, he may succeed in attaining his aim even by the methods he proposes, and we shall be willing to make the necessary arrangements for him to do so if he is prepared to take private lessons. Lest, however, he or anybody else should suppose that there is any merit, generally applicable, in the methods he proposes, we would point out that were his existing linguistic attainments to consist of a knowledge of Japanese and Russian, an acquirement of even that sort of knowledge of Italian which he wishes to possess would be absolutely impossible by his methods. Whereas if he would be willing to submit for a period of three months to the disciplines outlined in Part 3, up to the end of Stage 3, after which he might pass to graded texts dealing with economic subjects, he would be able to do what he wants to do, not only infinitely more effectively, but also for *any* existing language possessed of a Roman alphabet.

LETTER 4. THE READING OBJECTIVE

I must first beg you to excuse me for having let so much time pass before answering the letter in which you ask me how I wish to be taught Spanish. And yet I am glad I did not give an immediate answer, for in that case I should have said simply, 'Teach me Spanish in the way you think best', and have left it at that. A few days ago, however, I received from a friend of mine in America an educational review[1] in which appeared a digest of the views of Dr Michael West on the subject of language-study. I read it with intense interest, and was immediately convinced of the soundness of these views and the practicability of the method he suggests. In case you are not acquainted with Dr West's ideas I will set them forth succinctly here, with quotations.

Dr West starts by pointing out that we are losing a lot of time in modern language teaching, for three reasons: (*a*) we spend a great deal of time in practising things which we do not need; (*b*) we do not spend enough time practising the things that we do need; (*c*) we do not practise the things we need in order of importance.

Why are four hundred thousand American children learning French? If all these are really intending to visit France when they leave school, it seems to me that some one will have to get busy building more ships . . . Am I wrong in supposing that the dominant aim must be largely cultural—to get contact with French literature, and the culture of France? And if so, why all this emphasis on pronunciation, and the conversational lessons about buying

[1] *The Modern Language Forum.* Published by the Modern Language Association of Southern California, June 1931.

railway tickets? . . . Our course may aim primarily and essentially at the creation of reading ability in the language. This cuts out a good half or three-quarters of the grammar . . . and it cuts away two-fifths or a half of the vocabulary burden . . .

About three-quarters of your French enrolment is in the first two years. You can't learn to speak and write and read a language properly in two years. I gather from Professor Coleman's report[1] that some 160,000 children leave school every year with a mere smattering of French speech that cannot be much use to them. They can get no more than a mere 10 per cent. surrender value on their labours . . . I gather from my work during the past eight years with Indian pupils that a child learns to read a language about four times as fast as he learns to speak it.

Dr West goes on to give other and convincing reasons for the priority of reading, that a reading knowledge should be the first objective. Now, as a reading knowledge of Spanish is my only objective it is not surprising that I read with exceptional interest what Dr West recommends as a reading method. He goes on to say:

Is it possible to teach reading ability prior to and independent of speech ability? The ordinary view, of course, is that the best way of preparing a boy for reading is to teach him to speak. Now that seems to me on the face of it absurd. You are preparing him for something quite easy by teaching something which is at least four times more difficult, and so keeping down the progress of the reading course to one quarter of what it might be. It is like getting a baby to walk by teaching it roller-skating . . .

Our problem is to devise some system whereby a boy may learn to read. He must *learn to read by reading*. It is obvious that the crux of the whole problem is *the book*. For reading, a book is necessary; the boys can't read the teacher. The most that the teacher can do is to help the boys to read the book, and every single time the teacher opens his mouth, the boys (very correctly and politely) look up from their books—and stop reading! . . .

Reading, psychologically, is a process of sight-sound sense. (Sound may be actual speech, or merely auditory and kinaesthetic image.) In the early stages it is usually actual speech; but, when the child is able to read faster than he can speak—that is, over three hundred words a minute—speech begins to become a mere mutter, then a half-formed scheme or skeleton of words, and

[1] *The Teaching of Modern Foreign Languages in the United States,* by Algernon Coleman. Publications of the American and Canadian Committees on Modern Languages, vol. xii, New York, 1929.

eventually a silent shadow, passing through the mind with no outward show. It may even (possibly) drop out altogether, leaving a direct bond between sight and sense. Last of all we reach a stage at which the child is able to scan or skim.

Dr West then goes on to describe the reading-book, or series of reading-books, which will enable the child to develop in himself the psychological 'bonds' or skills described above, saying that he must pass through the stages in the order above described.

Such, in very condensed form, is Dr West's plan for the teaching of the reading of a foreign language.

I repeat, a reading knowledge of Spanish is my only objective, and therefore I would request you to teach me in such a way that I reach my objective without those needless *détours* into the fields of pronunciation, conversation, grammar, and written composition. I hope I am not too bold in referring you to the actual methods and procedures used by Dr West and by those American teachers who have been influenced by him and by the findings of Professor Coleman's report. For your guidance I append a bibliography of Spanish textbooks designed for reading-courses (this I have culled from the pages of the modern language review to which I alluded earlier).

Comments on Letter 4

There is a certain resemblance between the requirements and views of this correspondent and those of the prospective student of economic Italian. In both cases they look upon pronunciation, speech, grammar, and composition as needless *détours*; in both cases they assume that a reading knowledge of a foreign language is a special skill more or less unconnected with the other language skills, and independent of them.

Unlike our former correspondent, however, our prospective student of Spanish reading quotes in support of his plea the views of one of the foremost investigators in linguistic methodology, Dr Michael West, and sets forth his case with such a show of reason and reasonableness that at first sight it seems convincing.

At second sight it doesn't.

Let us say at once that our correspondent has presented us with nothing unfamiliar to us. We are well acquainted with Dr West's views and writings, and have often had occasion to admire and applaud his striking contributions to the science of linguistic methodology, and to agree with fully three-quarters of them.

One of Dr West's happiest inspirations is his *Principle of Specific Practice*. 'Find out what is your objective,' he says in effect, 'and aim solely at that objective, setting aside all things that do not lead to it.' In the present case he says in effect, 'If a reading knowledge is your objective, then do nothing that does not lead to that particular skill.'

In the brilliant article quoted by our correspondent there are, however, two statements that contradict each other, and the contradiction is of fundamental importance. In one place it is stated that we *learn to read by reading*, and that every time the teacher opens his mouth he is interrupting the process of reading, and thereby offending against the Principle of Specific Practice. In another place it is stated that reading is a process of 'sight-sound sense' (not merely of sight-sense, mark you, but of 'sight-*sound* sense'), and to emphasize the latter statement Dr West says that, although the 'sound' may be merely auditory and kinaesthetic image, it may be actual speech; *and in the early stages is usually actual speech!* (The italics and point of exclamation are ours.) Going still further, so that we may have not the shadow of doubt as to his meaning, he adds, a few lines after, that the child 'must pass through the stages in the order described', which can only mean that in the first stage the student *must learn to associate written symbols with actual speech.* Then if in the early stages reading is forming bonds between (*a*) the sight of the written word and (*b*) the fully articulated word, and (*c*) the sense of what is articulated, we fail to see why the voice of the teacher should act as an interruption of the process of reading. On the contrary, it looks as if the voice of the teacher were a necessary adjunct to the process of reading.

Dr West, we are sure, would agree with the following definition of the whole process of language-learning: *the fusing of linguistic symbols to the things they symbolize.*[1] His views will probably coincide with ours also in the following definition of the process of learning to read (for this is nothing other than an expansion of his own definition): *the fusing of the written words and at least of their acoustic-articulatory images to the notions for which they stand.*

Now what happens in actual practice when we start to read (or start to *learn* to read) a foreign language (and this foreign language may range between the two extremes of (*a*) an entirely strange and unfamiliar language and (*b*) a language rather similar in vocabulary and construction to one that is already familiar to us)? Let us see.

[1] For this definition and the conclusions that we draw from it we are indebted to the writer of Letter 11 in this Part.

Let us suppose that, as in the case of our correspondent, the reading skill is our sole objective; let us suppose that we are provided with one of the excellent Spanish textbooks referred to by our correspondent, this containing throughout its pages a number of explanatory pictures, and at the end a good Spanish-English vocabulary with phonetic notation. Let us suppose that Spanish is an entirely new language for us.

We try to read the first sentence, but are unable to do so because we do not know the meaning of the words contained in it.

H. E. P. (*interrupting the composition of these Comments*). But we could guess, and not be far wrong in our guess.

H. V. R. Yes, because we know French.

H. E. P. But if the text were devised very ingeniously, with pictures all over the place—

H. V. R. But if the language, instead of Spanish, were Czech or Finnish, or if the student were Chinese. Granting, however, that the text were so ingeniously composed, and so crawling with pictures that we could guess at some of the meaning, there would be, and must be— if not in the first sentence, in many of the subsequent sentences—a host of linguistic symbols we couldn't guess at.

H. E. P. But still—

H. V. R. All right, let's recast our last sentence as: 'We try to read the first sentences, but, in spite of the pictures that illustrate them, we are by no means sure of some of the words contained in them.'

H. E. P. Yes, that's clear enough. Let's go on. (*And we do.*)

So for a few moments we stop trying to read, and do something else instead: we refer to the vocabulary at the end of the book to discover the meaning of the unknown words (first offence against the Principle of Specific Practice). Then we turn again to the first sentences in order to read them.

But we must have some sort of notion as to how the words are pronounced, so we look up the phonetic transcription, or ask our teacher to pronounce them for us (second offence against the Principle of Specific Practice).

Having 'identified', so to speak, the meanings of the linguistic symbols, do we go on to the next sentence (or series of sentences)? Some probably would, but we don't. We feel that unless we fuse the various words (and other linguistic symbols) to the things they symbo- lize, we shall have all our work over again when we meet with them subsequently. So we stop and do one of two things: we either say (or think we are saying) the Spanish words and then say (or think we are saying) the corresponding English words, or we say (or think we are saying) the Spanish words while holding in our minds the notion for which they stand. (Never mind for the moment which is the right and which is the wrong procedure; and never mind for the moment what the exact nature of this fusing process is.) In either case we have stopped reading to do something else (third offence against the Principle of Specific Practice).

Some, maintaining that they remember words more easily by writing them down, will write down the sentence or sentences. (That will be a fourth offence against the Principle of Specific Practice.)

Others, maintaining that they remember words more easily by noting their etymology and syntactical peculiarities, will refer to a grammar book or big dictionary, and learn something about the sentences and the words contained in them. (That will be a fifth offence against the Principle of Specific Practice.)

Some of us will offend even more gravely against the principle. Convinced that such fusions as Spanish word—English word, or Spanish sentence—English sentence are the wrong sorts of fusions, and finding it an undue strain of attention to keep acoustic-articulatory images and the things symbolized by them in our mind (and this even in the case of an easy language like Spanish), we ask our teacher to articulate the sentences several times, and while doing so to make appropriate gestures to illustrate them and the words contained in them. In short, we ask him to help us out by giving us some oral-direct-method demonstration (and this is offending against the Principle of Specific Practice with a vengeance!).

But the time has come for us to interpret this principle less literally and more liberally. Let us define it as 'practice in the particular skill in which we are aiming to become proficient (e.g. reading) *and in any other skills that will contribute effectively to this end*', and immediately the Principle of Specific Practice is proof against such parodies and paradoxes as we have suggested above.

We will now return to the situation that presents itself when the student of a language unfamiliar to him sets out to learn to read it.

If he has had no linguistic training or experience—and especially if he is mentally sluggish, disliking effort, and not particularly keen on his work, he will do little but come to 'identify' the meanings of the words he sees. Instead of making efforts to create lasting bonds between the words and the things they symbolize, he will simply gaze at the text and wait for something to happen—and as he doesn't know anything of the language nothing is likely to happen.

If he has not been initiated into the technique of forming bonds between the words and the things for which they stand, he will probably content himself with forming bonds between the words and their supposed equivalents in his mother-tongue—a process of deciphering not reading.

H. E. P. (*interrupting again*). But you know that Sweet said that, when you really come to it,

Thing symbolized

Spanish symbol   *English symbol*

árbol =   = tree

for example, is much the same as

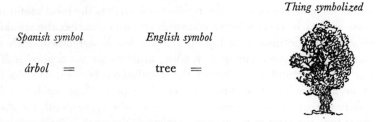

Thing symbolized

Spanish symbol   *English symbol*

árbol =   tree =

H. V. R. Yes, I know; and I've always felt there was something fallacious about the statement. It's because the example chosen is too glaringly concrete. I'm quite certain that, for example,

Spanish symbol	*Thing symbolized*	*English makeshift equivalent*
que aproveche =	[said to decline politely something proffered]	= may you relish it

is not at all the same as

Spanish symbol	English makeshift equivalent	Thing symbolized
que aproveche	= may you relish it	= [said to decline politely something proffered].

H. E. P. All right. Excuse the interruption. (*The interruption is excused, and the argument proceeds.*)

If the student has had training or experience, or if he is one of those who know by some sort of intuition what to do and what not to do in connexion with the learning of reading, he will proceed immediately first to 'identify' the unknown word (or whatever the linguistic symbol may be) and then to fuse it to its meaning by dint of articulation (or semi-articulation, or by kinaesthetic imagery) and of keeping his mind on the thing, action, circumstance, or situation for which the hitherto unknown symbol stands.

Our correspondent may have had this training or experience, or he may have the intuition, but there is something about his letter that suggests that he has not.

We are entirely in agreement with Dr West's statement that we are losing a lot of time in modern language-teaching—and for the three reasons that he gives. We are also fully in agreement that in certain countries or circumstances the reading objective is the most useful one (just as that in certain other countries or circumstances the speaking objective is the most useful one). We are less in agreement with the statement that the creation of reading ability cuts out a good half of the grammar and two-fifths of the vocabulary burden. We do not agree at all with the assumption that it is possible to teach reading ability prior to, and independent of, speech ability, nor with the statement that the crux of the whole problem is the book. (We must, after all, distinguish between reading and learning to read, as we must between speaking and learning to speak, or between translating and learning to translate, or between playing chess and learning to play chess.) If when the teacher opens his mouth the students stop reading, then also every time they look up or verify a meaning, a pronunciation, or a phenomenon of word-order they stop reading; and every time they pause or repeat in order better to fuse the word to its meaning, they stop reading!

Our correspondent refers to the many textbooks produced in recent years in America under the influence of the findings of Professor

Coleman's report. We possess several of these, and note that, although in them reading is stated to be the main or chief objective, more pages are devoted to grammar and tests than to the actual reading texts.

We suggest to our correspondent that he will find it more profitable, easier, and more interesting to follow for a period of from one to three months the programme outlined in Part 3, after which (Spanish being a comparatively easy language for English-speaking people) he will probably come to learn to read Spanish by reading it.

Yet one more point in answer to our correspondent: what is permissible, sound, and profitable to one who has been learning to read a foreign language for, say, three months (during which time he cannot have failed to learn much of the language itself) may be neither permissible, sound, nor profitable to a raw, undisciplined, and (linguistically speaking) ignorant beginner.

LETTER 5. FROM A STUDENT OF COMPARATIVE AND HISTORICAL PHILOLOGY

I am afraid that I do not fully grasp the implications of the letter that you have been good enough to send me, for you use terms that seem to me somewhat strange—or at least unfamiliar—in the present connexion. You speak of 'resistance' to 'disciplines', as if you were intending to impose a discipline on me and I were proposing to resist it.

It may be opportune if I state from the outset that I am unwilling to submit myself to any 'discipline' whatsoever, and if it is going to be a question of limiting my opportunities for scientific research on grounds of a normative discipline prescribed by pedagogues of the classical academic brand, I shall seek elsewhere the assistance that I require.

My mother-tongue is Finnish, and I possess two other languages (Swedish and Russian)—not to mention a working knowledge of German and English. I naturally know a good deal about Hungarian and Osmanli Turkish. I have studied Mongolian (written and spoken) in Mongolia, and residence in Japan has familiarized me with the elements of modern colloquial Japanese, and to some extent with the classical language in its written form.

My requirements are simple and easily satisfied. I wish to learn as much of Korean as will enable me to establish the relationship between Japanese and the Finno-Ugrian group of languages that has been my special subject of research. I am almost certain that Korean will provide the link. I have already found analogies between, on the one hand, Korean and Japanese, and, on the other, Korean and the languages of those peoples whose military emigrants peopled Turkey, Hungary, Estonia, and Finland, with their ancestral stock.

I desire to obtain reliable and first-hand information about Korean, not especially in regard to its phonetic system (I do not claim to be a phonetician except in so far as I use the phonetic transcription of the Swedish Dialect Society), but rather in regard to its general structure, and all of it that has successfully withstood first the Chinese, and more lately the Japanese, influence. I need to know little or nothing about those artificial and conventional phonetic adaptations of Chinese characters to fit in with the genius of the Korean language. Moreover, if your professor of Korean is going to occupy a large portion of the teaching hour in expatiating on 'things Korean', with an admixture of politics and archaeology, his lectures are going either to bore me or to make me laugh—for, without boasting, I may say that I know more than most people do about 'things Korean'.

Comments on Letter 5
Once again we have to deal with the case of a person who does not wish to learn a language in any comprehensive definition of the term. We do not mean by this that there is something illegitimate about his desires, but we should like to take this opportunity of protesting against the assumption, so often made, that a desire such as this is somehow infinitely more legitimate than that of a man who wishes to learn a language for waiting at table in a French-speaking *milieu*. As a matter of fact, to the comprehensive language-course planner, our friend here is a nuisance in the same way as the prospective waiter is a nuisance. And we feel sorely tempted to hand him over to the quacks, as the prospective waiter-linguist is by most seats of learning in the world. But we shall not do so. We shall say to him, 'Sir, we can cater for you in our course of Korean Historical Grammar and Philology, which will be conducted in English. As you don't want to learn the language, but only to learn about the language, it certainly doesn't matter to us in what language you do it. If, sir, however, you attempt to dignify your peculiar needs to the level of desirable linguistic standards, and try to make us—or anybody else—believe that what you are undertaking is a normal and scholarly course in Korean, we *shall* consign you to the quacks, for the study of foreign languages has already suffered far too long from this particular sort of idiosyncrasy.

LETTER 6. FROM AN ACCOMMODATING STUDENT OF RIPER YEARS

As 'a prospective language student of riper years', as you put it, who wishes to take up the study of Dutch (or rather Netherlandish), I note with interest what you express as a confession, and view with sympathy what you express as a doubt. I take it that you are asking me what I want and how I want it put across.

The answer is quite simple. I want to learn what the English call Dutch, and I want to have you put it across in such a way that I learn it with a maximum of success and a minimum of drudgery. I want to become able to read Dutch and to write it and to make myself intelligible to those whose mother tongue it is, in Holland and elsewhere, and I want to become able to understand what they say when they speak to me—and when they speak to each other in my hearing.

How you are going to do that is up to you. If it is my business to learn it is your business to know how to cause me to learn. It is because I trust you to do your part of the business that I am applying to you, and not the Oxford Street language school people for help. To which of the linguistic disciplines am I willing to submit myself? I am willing to submit myself to the linguistic disciplines that you prescribe, just as I am willing to submit myself to the hygienic disciplines that my medical adviser prescribes. Similarly, if I go to law I place myself unreservedly in the hands of my solicitor. Similarly, as a Catholic, I place my conscience in the hands of the Mother Church, whose business it is to be the keeper of my conscience.

As I am not going to give any hints to my medico, my lawyer, or my priest, as to how they shall prescribe for my physical, financial, or spiritual well-being, so I refrain from advising my linguistic advisers. When one keeps a dog to do the barking one does not bark oneself: this on the grounds of common sense, of economics, and of logic.

You just teach me what the English call Dutch, and use those methods that you consider most appropriate for the purpose. If you succeed (and I see no reason why you should not succeed) I shall be able within the next year or two to express in Dutch what I am endeavouring in the course of this letter to express in English.

Comments on Letter 6

If our correspondent does not modify his attitude towards his linguistic advisers as a result of his first six hours' studies in our institute there will be satisfaction on both sides. He will get what he wants, and we shall give him what he wants—viz. Dutch 'as speech'. We fear, however, that he will resist some of our disciplines because in the field of linguistics every person is conscious of one accomplishment—that of possessing his own language 'as speech', which he feels—unconsciously perhaps—entitles him to an opinion as to how another language is to be acquired. Our correspondent cites his religious humility as a parallel, but he has never got on terms—speaking or other—with any god up to the time he places himself in the hands of the priest. If he had he might be critical and a resister—as he will almost certainly be in relation to our teaching disciplines for Dutch. All of which goes to show that what is really required is the recognition of linguistics as a definite branch of science protected by the sacerdotalism attached to the medical profession, for example. The difficulty that we are going to have with this prospective student is a difficulty caused by the general lack of recognition of linguistic pedagogy as a science. Learners, teachers, and others who should know better deem the necessary equipment of the language-teacher to be simply a knowledge of the language he proposes to teach. The result is that the world is filled with competent language-knowers who are grossly incompetent language-teachers dealing with an even vaster army of cantankerous (often justifiably so) language-learners, the one group entirely ignorant of what they *should* teach, and the other of what they *would* learn.

At this juncture the commentators discarded the pen for the tongue and said:

H. E. P. Do you know, Redman, the last two sentences crystallize what has been worrying me for at least the past twenty-five years? All the trouble that I have had with my adult language students plus all the trouble I have had with my language teachers, the emotional resistances and all those frictions that are found in the foreign language classroom (and, apparently, in no other classroom)—all this is explained in those last two sentences. They constitute more than an explanation; they are a diagnosis.

H. V. R. I'm not sure if this isn't the most important part of the whole of this language-learning business. You're looking round for somebody to blame, and as a teacher you naturally blame your *vis-à-vis*, the pupil. He's not respectful enough. He doesn't recognize you as an expert, any more than the man who asks another the way to Oxford Circus recognizes the fellow who knows as an expert. This fellow happens to know the way to Oxford Circus, and *you* happen to know the language.

To suggest that the inquirer should take a bus is impertinence; he always travels by taxi. You're there to give the student the information, but not to tell him the way to go. But his attitude is not his fault. The fault is with the people who, as we said just now, should know better— viz. the educationists, who suppose that language-knowing is the only necessary qualification for language-teaching. Has it ever struck you that anybody who has ever made a contribution to language-teaching technique has at the outset been looked upon either as a quack, as was the case with Berlitz and Gouin (hardly respectable in academic circles, don't you know?), or regarded as a fanatic, like Sweet, whose incursions into the field of linguistic pedagogy were made respectable only by the fact that he knew half a dozen languages?

H. E. P. But surely all this *is* recognized, even if only in a vague way. How can we explain the attitude of disdain towards the 'native teacher' except by the assumption that he provides nothing except his know-ledge of his language? He is the tame foreigner whose only teaching qualification is the fact that he was born in the country of his mother-tongue. But what does he know of English, French, Arabic, etc., who only English, French, Arabic, etc., knows? It is felt that he cannot look upon his mother-tongue from the point of view of the students who are to learn it, and so he is not taken too seriously. All this points to the fact that it is the 'how to teach' that counts far more than the 'what to teach'.

H. V. R. It points to absolutely nothing of the sort. The non-employment of the 'native' simply points to the fact that the attitude towards language-learning in the majority of our institutions is that it should aim at extension of the mother-tongue. The teacher whose native language is that of the student, having *learned* the foreign language, as it is called, certainly knows quite a lot about it in relation to the native language, but to know one sort of thing in relation to another sort of thing does not involve knowledge of how to teach one or the other. The joke of the whole thing is that these fellows don't even know how to translate: all their translation experience was gained when they were using translation as an instrument for learning the foreign language—which makes it useless for any other purpose including, of course, the real purpose of translation.

H. E. P. I'm not quite sure whether I understand what you're driving at.

H. V. R. I'm driving particularly at the fellows who are remarkably competent at explaining that *Je veux que vous fassiez cela* means 'I want that you do that', and who are yet incapable of any sort of translation which goes beyond that limit. Ask them for the translation of *Je n'y suis pour rien dans l'affaire*, and they'll find 'It's no use blaming me' in a month of February the 29ths, but will be singularly adept in explaining that this slightly exotic 'idiom' means 'I am there for nothing (in the affair).' All of which boils the whole question down to this: they have not realized, nor have they been taught to realize, that translation is a process of thinking consecutively with two different languages. They have been taught to think about French with English, and they do so with an ingenuity worthy of a better cause. The question that all our educationists have never answered honestly is, Do you want your students to learn French or simply to learn how French differs from English (or whatever the foreign or native language may be)? It is because the native teacher introduces, not the 'queer' element, but the 'natural' (and slightly incomprehensible) element into the classroom that he is suspect in a certain measure—and is to be replaced, as soon as possible, by one who teaches French, not so much *as* French, but as a foreign language (with every emphasis on the *foreign*).

H. E. P. I wonder.

H. V. R. You've no need to wonder. It's the easist thing in the world to put to the test. Just go and apply for a position as a teacher of foreign languages anywhere in Europe. Germany, France, and Italy will, as you say, turn you down because you're not a national. In England they will ask you about (*a*) your modern language degree, (*b*) your experience abroad; and that's all. If you fulfil their requirements in these respects, and there's a post vacant, you'll get it—and it won't matter twopence whether you've any experience in teaching the language you propose to teach, or, alternatively, any theoretical knowledge of the way to teach it. In a word, you will be engaged on what you *know*; the assumption being that if you know some French or German—or whatever it may be—you will soon tumble to the teaching part, *tant bien que mal*. And you wonder that adult students don't respect your judgment as to teaching your own subject. If they sin they sin in very good company—that of university senates, appointments boards, education committees, and eminent headmasters, who all consider knowledge of a language the only *sine qua non* of a language teacher.

H. E. P. Yes, you're probably right—worse luck!

H. V. R. I'm certainly right. It is true that nowadays the Normal Schools pretend to give you some training in methodology, but it

amounts to very little. It consists simply of general training in education on the one hand, and, on the other, of training in the mechanical
translation habits to which we have referred. There's absolutely
nothing to be done by language teachers as a body until it is generally
recognized that the capacity to teach a language is at least as important
as a knowledge of it.

H. E. P. 'Mechanical translation habits', you said. As I see it, the
term 'mechanical' is taboo in the educational circles of today. The
educational world in Japan, as in America and England and Europe
in general stresses the fact that, however we teach the foreign language,
we must not teach it by methods that savour of the mechanical—that
we are not parrot-trainers, as the Victorians were. In my efforts in
Japan, as elsewhere, I have been told that we are past the age of
educating by mechanical methods. Nearly all the resistance that I
have encountered in striving to introduce common-sense procedures
has been accompanied by the comment that the mechanical is out of
date.

H. V. R. It may be out of date in other educational fields, but it's very
much in date in conventional language-teaching. Whether it's the
reform-method people who insist on the necessity for a thorough
grounding in elementary grammar-mechanisms, or our predecessors
who insisted on a machine-like type of what they called 'translation',
it's the mechanical all the time. The old-timer mechanist calls the new-
time variety a mere mechanist—a variation of the pot calling the kettle
black. The old and the new are at one in insisting that certain things
linguistic can be accomplished only by the aid of mechanics—we differ
only in our selection of those things that must be learnt, or taught, by
that aid.

LETTER 7. A TYPICAL HEADMASTER (OR PRINCIPAL) REPLIES
I am particularly glad to receive your letter because it puts to me the
very question which I feared that you, as specialists in the teaching of
language, would overlook.

I prefer, if I may, to divide my answer to your question as to the
reasons for which I wish my boys to be taught French into three parts.
The first and most obvious reason is that they may be able to pass
the examination for the School Leaving Certificate, preferably sufficiently well to obtain at the same time the Matriculation Certificate of

the University of London. You are doubtless familiar with the nature of the examination that they will have to undergo. They will be required to answer certain questions on French grammar, which will necessitate their being familiar with the contents of an average secondary-school French grammar-book, such as Heaths'.[1] Moreover, they will be required to do two pieces of translation, into and out of French respectively, and a piece of free composition in French, and finally to submit to a short oral test of their ability to read aloud, write dictation, and converse in French. I must confess, however, that I do not feel that these considerations need preoccupy you to any considerable extent in the planning of your course of study; for my experience is that proficiency in the art of passing this examination—whether or not it may be called proficiency in French—can be attained by any boy of average intelligence in a year, by whatever methods he has been previously instructed, and even if he has not been instructed at all. Nevertheless it will be necessary for you to make provision in the last year for the requirements of this examination.

As for the rest, there are two main reasons for which my boys are learning French, the second of which is infinitely more important than the first. The first is purely a utilitarian one. Ten per cent of our boys will go on to the university, and of these approximately 10 per cent will pursue their studies of French—that is to say, will put to use, in acquiring knowledge of French literature, French history, and French philology, the knowledge of the language which you have been able to give them. Practically speaking, then, there is a necessity for you to prepare 1 per cent of the boys for subsequent advanced studies of the language—the rest of the university-goers, for one purpose or another will probably have to maintain a nodding acquaintance with the language, in order to read texts in their various specialist subjects. The remaining 90 per cent will enter some sort of business, and of these it can safely be said that not more than 10 per cent will require to use their French for purposes of commercial correspondence or for business conversations with French-speaking peoples. Roughly, then, there are 19 per cent, or shall we say 20, of all our boys who will put their French to some utilitarian purpose, and this purpose is essentially different in each of the three cases I have described. Moreover, when a boy enters the school and begins learning French we do not know whether he is destined to become one of the 80 per cent, or one of the 20 per cent, but some sort of French has to be taught to him.

[1] *Heath's New Practical French Grammar*, by W. H. Fraser and J. Squair. Harrap, 1922.

This brings me conveniently to my next division. The essential reason for which French appears on the school curriculum is a cultural one. We wish the pupils' French-learning to assist in the general process of educating them. We feel that the learning of a modern language provides an educational discipline, if not equal to that of classical studies, at any rate of essentially the same nature. In their study of the structure of the language the pupils will learn much of the structure of language in general, and incidentally of their own language in particular. In their study of new forms of expression they will enrich their intellectual experience and hence increase their power of expression in their own language. To a limited extent, too, they will come into contact with the way of life and thought of another and a great people; and this contact, limited though it is, cannot but be of value in broadening the mind—in short, it has an educative value. I do not stress this, because all my experience tells me that in the majority of cases this contact is only very slightly made in the secondary schools, but, on the other hand, I do feel that all the language-learning which our pupils are getting is giving them an extension of linguistic possibilities, and hence of their mother-tongue. Kipling's question hurled at the stay-at-home Briton is equally applicable to those devoid of a knowledge, however scanty, of foreign languages: 'What should they know of English who only English know?'

The complete answer that I have given to your first question makes it considerably easier to answer the second, How do you wish this French to be taught, with particular reference to disciplines? I take it that by this word 'discipline' you mean what the layman would describe as method. As I have said, the only general reason for learning French which our pupils have is the cultural one, which I have briefly, but I think adequately, described above. This being the case I should naturally prefer the methods employed to serve as far as possible the aim in view. You are probably thinking of my attitude towards direct method procedures, oral method procedures, and the use of phonetics. I have no objection to the use of direct and oral methods, but, on the other hand, I should like to say frankly that I have no particular enthusiasm for them. You will claim—and I shall not dispute your claim for a moment—that they make for efficient language-learning, that students taught by such methods will possess a superior knowledge of French to that of those taught by other methods. But, as you will have gathered, I am not primarily concerned with my pupils' acquirement of efficiency in French, because, as we have seen, only 20 per cent of them really need to acquire that efficiency. On the other hand, I know that translation methods are going to increase their knowledge of, and capacity to use effectively, their own language, which is a necessity for them all. I know also that grammar methods are going to give them a training in logical classification, of educative value in itself, and an acquaintance with the structure of language generally, which will (*a*) give them confidence in the manipulation of their own language, and (*b*) make the subsequent learning of another European language a relatively easy matter.

By insistence on direct and oral methods I fear that, to a greater or lesser extent, the educative processes of the older methods are to be sacrificed. You may be able to put forward a claim that the direct and oral methods inculcate other general disciplines of as great an educative value as those I have described. If so I shall be happy to learn of them. But I fear that you will not put forward any such claims. You will take your stand on efficiency, purely linguistic efficiency, and that is the difference between the specialist and the general educator. You are in the fortunate position of being able to pursue language for language's sake. But as far as my pupils are concerned, it must be pursued rather for education's sake.

What I have said with regard to direct and oral methods applies with equal force to the study of phonetics. Other things being equal, I want my boys to have a good French pronunciation, just as I wish them to have a sound knowledge of the language. But in the allocation of time I wish it to be kept constantly in mind that every process must serve for general education, and that if it does not so serve its use should be reduced to a minimum.

I hope I have made myself clear. I am perfectly willing for my boys to be submitted to the modern linguistic disciplines provided that those other disciplines of proven educative value are not entirely ignored. I go even further and say that if the new linguistic disciplines can be shown to have an educative value apart from their value in teaching the language, then I am willing for my boys to be submitted to them to the exclusion of the others. That is my attitude fully expressed, an attitude shared, I venture to think, by most enlightened secondary school headmasters today.

Comments on Letter 7
We have made ample provision for the examination requirements of our correspondent's charges, so we can safely take it that his first

paragraph is disposed of. For the 20 per cent of his pupils who wish to continue their studies of French there will also be no difficulty; they will get what they want and probably more than they or their head-master expect.

For the 80 per cent who don't want to learn French at all as a unit of their studies, but merely as an extension of their mother-tongue, we have to give more careful thought. Reluctantly we shall have to admit that we shall not give satisfaction to these pupils—or rather to our correspondent, who claims to interpret their requirements. French, in the way we intend to teach it, will not serve as an extension of the mother-tongue. We should like to add, in passing, that it seems rather strange that extension of the mother-tongue should be pursued in the French classroom. It seems almost like giving the mathematics master a free hand to inculcate mathematics to the best of his ability provided that the pupils get a good knowledge of geography at the same time. In a word, just as we feel that it is thoroughly pernicious to teach French through English, we can and will give no undertaking to teach English through French.

We are glad to receive the invitation to justify modern methods of linguistic pedagogy on purely general grounds. We would do so here but for the fact that we have received by the same post another letter from another enlightened—possibly a more enlightened—headmaster on this very subject. We might refer our correspondent, then, to the letter immediately following this, particularly to the passage which begins, 'I hope that you will teach modern languages as Latin has been taught in my school up to the present—that is to say, by the direct method.'

If, in spite of our insistence on teaching one language properly, in a certain classroom, rather than half teaching two, our correspondent is still disposed to send us his charges, we shall put them through the normal course up to the end of Stage 5, and in Stage 6 give them free composition, translation, and translation-grammar.

LETTER 8. ANOTHER ACADEMIC ATTITUDE

You are right in supposing that I regard the study of foreign languages as of sufficient importance to justify my placing my charges in your expert hands. My feeling on this subject being so strong, I am reluctant even to appear to prescribe in any way what form that language instruction should take. You say that it is my business to co-ordinate the instruction which my pupils receive in their various subjects in such a way as to ensure their acquirement of a balanced education. This may be so, but I do not feel myself called upon to tell my teacher of history what sort of history he shall teach (beyond, of course, saying that it shall be English history or French history, as the case may be) or how he shall teach it. Indeed as I look down the whole curriculum I see no subject in regard to which I am called upon to give such definite commands. I have been taught to regard my teachers as experts in their own subjects, and therefore I consider that methods can safely be left to them.

When you ask me what *kind* of French and German I want taught I almost feel like answering facetiously and saying, 'The French kind', or 'The German kind', as the case may be. But I take it that you are really asking, what are the purposes for which our boys are learning modern languages, in order that you may be guided by those purposes in the choice of methods and material, and also in the emphasis which shall be placed on this or that aspect of the language you teach. Now our boys have as many different reasons for learning French, for example, as they have for learning geometry. Some of them may become architects and actually require the geometry they have learned. Others may enter firms having dealings with French-speaking peoples, become diplomats, enter those branches of the Civil Service in which French is required, or become teachers of French or husbands of French women—in all of which cases they will find their French extremely useful. But we don't know any of these things in advance, and so in drawing up our educational budget it would be futile to make provision for any one of these eventualities, though we must, of course, make slight provision for them all. And in making that provision we must be careful to ensure that, even if the knowledge acquired by the boy—be it geometry or German—is never to be of any practical use at all, it shall at least have assisted him to a realization that knowledge is an aid not only to getting a living, but also to living *tout court*.

This leads me to say, then, that the purposes for which I want French and German taught are all the purposes for which French and German are ever taught. These are classified and set forth admirably in the findings of the Committee on the Position of Modern Languages in the Educational System of Great Britain, published in 1918 under the title of *Modern Studies*. I must confess frankly that I do not see what those purposes have to do with you. There are so many purposes for which our boys might use the French they learn that you cannot possibly take them into consideration in the designing of your courses. After all, I might have done better if I had stopped at my facetious injunction at the beginning of the last paragraph and said, 'Teach the French kind of French, and that's all.'

I said earlier on that I felt myself neither competent nor justified to prescribe methods in a sphere of instruction outside my personal knowledge. Since, however, your letter requires an answer, I may perhaps permit myself the luxury of expressing a few hopes. I hope that you will teach modern languages as Latin has been taught in my school up to the present—that is to say, by the direct method. We were induced to employ this method for the teaching of Latin by the success attained by Dr Rouse and his colleagues at the Perse School, Cambridge.

The accounts of Dr Rouse's transformation of school work at the classics read like a romance. He speaks of 'the extraordinary effect on the learner in keeping his attention and goodwill. Their memories of their work are pleasant. They are glad to have done it. For the pupil, the direct method, which may appear superficially to make his work easy, really makes him willing to do it. There is more real hard work than under the indirect system, but it is done with the same zest as his games are played, and it leaves him with a consciousness of power.' His boys make Greek and Latin speeches before their fellows, they produce plays, some of them home-made, they write letters and short stories, they bandy wit in Greek and Latin. The number of hours spent on Latin at the public schools before the sixth form he estimates at 2,160; on his [i.e. Dr Rouse's] direct method lines he spends 613.[1]

This might serve as an almost exact account of our experience here. We find that our teaching of the classics by the direct method is productive, not only of intrinsically better results, but also of an attitude of enthusiasm towards classical studies which I venture to think unparalleled in the schools of this country where the subjects are taught by the traditional methods. This experiment has taught us something more; it has shown us that the disciplines associated with the direct method (in that they are different from the disciplines associated with other methods) make for a more balanced mental training. The disciplines employed in the old-style Latin classroom were in no wise

[1] *Modernism in Language Teaching*, edited by H. E. Moore.

different from those of the history classroom or the geography classroom, whereas the direct method disciplines furnish a training which cannot be acquired in the course of learning other subjects, and therefore have a very peculiar general educative value apart from their intrinsic value in language instruction. Now, if this is possible for Latin it must be infinitely more possible and desirable for living languages, and I therefore sincerely hope that you will employ this method in your teaching of French and German.

For very much the same reasons I hope that you will give adequate attention to phonetics. It is not only that, other things being equal, it is desirable that language-learners should have a reasonably accurate pronunciation rather than an atrocious one, but other inestimable advantages are to be gained. Phonetics teaches auditory observation, oral imitation, and also the relation between sounds and their physiological instruments. Above all, it gives the learner a new vision of all the phenomena of speech-sounds. It rids him of the age-long artificial association between the sounds he utters and the conventional alphabets and orthographies which usually symbolize them, and which symbolize them so inadequately or falsely that his whole conception of pronunciation phenomena is distorted by them. It enables him to *see*, not only the foreign language, but also his mother-tongue, and to see them, not through the spectacles of those for whom a language is nothing but a spelling-system, but as they really are. In a word, it releases him from the tyranny of the letter, and this is more than a discipline: it is an education, and a liberating, and therefore liberal, education at that.

Finally, I hope that if you find it necessary or desirable to teach grammar you will teach it in such a way as to train the reason rather than the memory, analytically rather than mechanically, in terms of substitution tables rather than in those of philology. Moreover, I hope that grammar will be taught solely for the purpose of overcoming difficulties, and not to create new ones—as is so often the case at the present time.

These are a few random suggestions which may be of service to you, but I should like to say once again, in conclusion, that I am putting my boys in the hands of linguistic experts because I feel that, unlike the teaching of other subjects in our secondary schools, the teaching of languages has been mainly in the hands of non-experts—not through any fault of language teachers as such, but through a general belief that expertness is not required in this field. This being the case, I want to assure you again that I give you the same liberty of action that tradition demands I should give the other experts under my supervision.

Comments on Letter 8
This headmaster fortunately relieves us of the necessity of making any special provision for specific needs. He realizes that the absurdity of a specialized approach to language is as great as that of a specialized approach to any of the subjects on the curriculum. Desirous as we are of inculcating a general attitude towards language—viz. the 'as speech' attitude—we should be seriously handicapped if we had to deal with specialized demands at the very outset of our teaching.

As far as methods are concerned, we feel that he will find all he wants and more, in the course outlined in Part 3. Incidentally, he furnishes a revealing answer to the other distinguished member of his profession who asks what general educative disciplines can be derived from modern methods. We are indeed tempted to send this letter to our correspondent No. 7, in the hope that it may convince him that his views are not so entirely representative of those held by enlightened headmasters of today as he imagines.

Our correspondent here speaks at some length of the peculiar educative disciplines of direct and oral methods, pointing out their distinctive character from those inculcated by the teaching of other subjects. It might be well to list those distinctive disciplines here. The oral method gives a training in observation, imitation, confidence, and readiness in expression, in so far at least as linguistic activities are concerned. The direct method (in its dual form, the ostensive and the contextual) gives a training in observation, the capacity to analyse complicated thought into simpler elements, and the capacity to seek simple definitions rather than to accept labels. A pupil who has received language-teaching by the contextual direct method forms the habit of making a simplifying paraphrase of complicated words or expressions. This habit of paraphrase develops into a habit of analysis and definition, and thus he thinks of words and phrases in terms of their simpler definitions. In short, they come to represent very precise meanings to him, rather than vague gestures towards meaning, as is the case with most of us in relation to so many of the words and expressions which we use constantly.

4

LETTER 9. FROM A PRACTICAL PARENT

In reply to your letter asking me for what purpose I wish my sons to learn German I should like to say that it is my intention to take them into my business, where they will be required to handle German commercial correspondence. It will be necessary for them to understand the letters they receive from time to time, to make rapid and accurate translations of descriptive catalogues, etc., and to be able to reply to letters in German. They will never be required to write any sort of German but commercial German, and they will never be required to *speak* German at all.

I think I have made their requirements pretty clear, but I am afraid I don't understand very well your question about disciplines. I take it that you will teach them enough of the grammar of the language to enable them to write accurately, that you will give them a good general vocabulary, and as much commercial vocabulary as the conditions of your classes permit. I hope I am as reasonable as most people. I do not expect you to teach them commercial terms all the time, but I would beg you, when arranging for their classes, to have their ultimate aims always in view. I should never protest against a reasonable amount of general instruction in the language, as long as it is practical, non-literary, and non-conversational. The word 'conversational' reminds me that I should complain if a lot of their time were taken up with oral work which would never be of the slightest value to them. The same applies to phonetics, which, in addition to being useless, will, I am told—and it seems to me a reasonable statement— seriously affect their capacity to spell with ordinary German orthography. I think that is all I have to say. As long as you are teaching them to write correctly, translate quickly and accurately, and read easily, we shall not quarrel. If you go in for spoken German, literary German, abstruse German grammar, or phonetics, they will be getting what they don't want, and I shall kick.

Comments on Letter 9

The statement of aims which our correspondent has made is clear and concise; these we understand and appreciate, and we feel that we can provide for them.

The statement of resistances is the usual muddle, and before stating what we shall do for our correspondent's sons we feel that the muddle must be cleared up. He says that he wishes the material to be non-literary, and here he is voicing a resistance, which many pupils and parents must have felt, to the fantastic texts which have been used for language-teaching in secondary schools for many years past. If he means by 'non-literary' texts which shall be clear, and composed of neutral vocabulary—that is to say, vocabulary which would be equally appropriate in most other texts—then there will be no kicking or quarrelling on either side. The language material used must be also non-conversational, says our correspondent. If he means by 'non-conversational' material that is not exclusively colloquial, but belongs to both the spoken and the written language, again there need be no friction between us. The word 'conversational' leads him to 'oral', which it shouldn't. He seems to think that oral work is of no assistance to proficiency in written work—as if an oral repetition of the seven times table were of no help to a bank clerk drawing up an annual balance-sheet. If his young people find their way into our institute quite a lot of their time will be taken up with oral work, and it will be of the greatest value to them in making them, not mechanical little *speakers* of German, but natural little *writers* of German. Our correspondent—to judge by his communication—is a fluent writer of English. It might be suggested to him that his writing would be considerably less fluent if he couldn't speak English.

When our correspondent is convinced of the value of oral work as a training for natural and effective writing—and one so sweetly reasonable will, we feel sure, not fail to be convinced in a very short time— his objection to phonetics will also be dissipated. Our experience has shown us that a considerable proportion of spelling mistakes, made when writing the foreign language, are due to the vague acoustic image possessed by the writer. To take a common example in our present environment, a Japanese frequently writes *l* for *r*, or vice versa, in an English word, for the natural and simple reason that no distinction is made in Japanese between the sounds *l* and *r*. That distinction can be given to him only by adequate phonetic training. Our correspondent's objection to phonetics on the grounds of causing confusion with conventional orthography is, of course, in reality an objection to the use of phonetic symbols. The language happening to be German (and not French, English, or Danish), and German orthography being on the whole regular and consistent, we should not, in any case, propose to make an extensive use of phonetic symbols.

What, then, shall the prescribed course be? Up to Stage 5 these pupils will follow the normal course without any deviation. In Stage 5 certain of the reading-texts will contain vocabulary suitable for commercial purposes. In Stage 6 the pupils will take the course in commercial correspondence and also the course in general translation.

LETTER 10. FROM A PARENT WHO WANTS TO UTILIZE THE NATURAL LANGUAGE-LEARNING FORCES

The substance of my reply to your courteous communication is contained in an article that I contributed recently to the columns of a well-known educational journal. In it I have expressed my views on an aspect of language-learning that seems to have escaped the notice of most of those who write on the subject. As I have a dislike for saying the same thing twice over I am taking the liberty of sending you a cutting from the journal in question, and I would beg you to consider it as if were a personal communication to you.

[And this is the cutting.]

At an extremely early age we became able to understand what was said to us and to make ourselves understood by those who constituted our environment. No matter what the language, no matter how great its phonetic or grammatical complexity, within a couple of years of our birth we were able to use it as a medium of communication. We acquired this capacity without conscious effort, without lessons or study in the ordinary sense of these terms. Before the age of two we were able to listen with understanding to the telling of stories; to associate with whatever meaning they may have, and to repeat with glee and enthusiasm, the nursery rhymes of our childhood. Perhaps at this same early age we found ourselves in two different linguistic environments, one parent speaking to us in one language, and the other in another. We tackled the two languages with equal facility, rarely if ever mixing them. In the literal sense of the term, language-learning was child's play.

In no other subject of learning do we find any parallel. With the exception of the child prodigy, we find no examples of babies becoming proficient in the exercise of a series of complicated mental processes comparable with those associated with language. At the age of two we do not spontaneously and successfully perform arithmetical operations, nor exhibit proficiency in chess-playing or map-making. We are not yet even able to perform that operation known as telling the time.

Let us compare the tremendous degree of success that attended our first efforts to learn our own language with that which attended our first efforts, ten or twenty years later, to learn some other language. Look at English Johnny at the age of twelve, wrestling with the mystery of French; see him struggling with the French verb; note the errors in his compositions, his barbarous pronunciations, his bewilderment when addressed in French. On the other hand, look at French Alphonse, who at the age of three is a master in French in so far as its vocabulary and style are appropriate to his age. But Johnny gets his own back when, a few years later, Alphonse starts learning Johnny's language. Look at Alphonse in his efforts to make head or tail of English even in the regularized form in which it is presented to him. And yet if we could cause an English Johnny and a French Alphonse to become playmates at the age of three, within a few weeks either Johnny would be using natural and fluent French or Alphonse would be using natural and fluent English, or perhaps both would happen. *Robinson Crusoe* is a wonderful book, but a real Friday would have learned to speak Robinson Crusoe's English, and not his Carib adaptation of it.

I could write in this vein page after page, and accumulate example after example, all taken from real life and personal experience, examples taken from my own trilingual family, examples taken from the experience of people who have constituted my daily environment in three different countries during the past thirty years.

Need I do so? I think not.

May we not, without further evidence, legitimately claim that we are all endowed with certain natural linguistic powers, that man is born with an innate capacity for speech, with a power analogous to (but not identical with) the power of walking, of eating and drinking? Walking, eating, and other primitive activities are ranged among the instincts, and if the capacity for using language is not among them it is something not far removed from them—probably what McDougall terms an 'impulse'.

We are endowed by nature with certain linguistic powers. Of this we are certain, for if we were not so endowed our speech accomplishments would be rather in the nature of miracles than normal phenomena. They are strange powers, powers of which little is known but their potency and effects.

Given the right opportunities we may develop, encourage, and strengthen these powers; bereft of such opportunities, these powers will be weakened, discouraged, inhibited, or even destroyed. The child in his natural environment has every opportunity of strengthening them; the student in classroom conditions as we know them today has every inducement to ignore them, to discredit them, and to destroy them. The opportunities in question are those of hearing the language, imitating the spoken word, and associating the spoken word with the thing that it symbolizes. Give the student opportunities for hearing and imitating the spoken words associated with those gestures and contexts that they symbolize; give him these opportunities in rapid succession, not limiting them to conventional, grammatical, or other categories, but providing them abundantly and generously, unhampered by traditional limitations; never mind whether the word or expression is regular or irregular;

give the raw material unstintingly and always associated with the thought content of this material. By so doing will you develop the natural powers of speech.

What are some of the things that inhibit these natural powers? Among them are to be counted what are called 'explanations'. The average teacher tends to 'explain' (in the student's mother-tongue, of course) all the unfamiliar words and expressions occurring in the foreign text. Each such explanation, if clearly and accurately given, does indeed cause the learner to understand more about the language, but at the same time it tends to inhibit the natural powers of language-learning. With each explanation in the mother-tongue the learner will tend to rely more and more on explanations and less and less on his own powers.

Translation is another of those things that, while increasing the learner's skill in one direction—the analytic study of the language—decreases his power of direct and spontaneous understanding.

'Deciphering' is the name of that process by which we worry out the meaning of a difficult text by dint of grammatical and etymological analysis, and without reference to the thought content of that text. This deciphering is another of the things that make the learner skilful in one direction at the expense of skill in another, and generally more important, direction. When the explanations, translations, and deciphering proceed at a slow rate this slowness in itself discourages the student in his efforts to utilize these natural powers.

Let me give an analogy. We are all endowed with natural capacities for good health. Drugs are auxiliaries to good health, but an abuse of them will decrease the curative powers of nature. Here is a patient who suffers from insomnia. He takes a sleeping-draught and he sleeps; the draught has indeed given him sleep, but it has diminished in a certain degree the power of natural sleep. The more he drugs the better does he sleep—but the less is is able to sleep without drugs.

So with language-learning. Explanations, translations, and the like are the drugs. Each one helps the student to understand or to compose, and each dose makes it more difficult for the student to utilize his nature-given capacities for language-learning.

And what are the things that encourage, develop, and strengthen these powers? One of them is the existence of conditions in which the learner cannot but associate the word with the thing that the word stands for: the opportunity to hear the word 'tree' while contemplating a tree; the opportunity to hear the words 'thank you' in conditions that call for the act of thanks. Another is hearing continuously the foreign language spoken by one who is able to make himself understood by means of gestures, actions, objects, pictures, etc. Another is giving continual opportunities and encouragements to imitate or to reproduce what has been heard; another, continual opportunities for constructing sentences (or portions of sentences) on the analogy of sentences (or portions of them) previously acquired. Another consists in speed and variety of procedures.

All of these things strengthen our natural language-learning capacities just as the other things mentioned previously tend to weaken them.

Having pointed out the existence of these natural and spontaneous powers, and having proved, as I hope, that they are the only things that we learn our mother-tongue with, I now suggest that it is reasonable to utilize these same powers for learning the foreign language.

Whether we use them to the exclusion of all other instruments of language-study or whether we use them in combination with processes and procedures other than those dictated by nature, is a point open to discussion, but to ignore the existence of these powers, or to refuse to consider them in connexion with the foreign language course, can be interpreted only as a disregard of all dictates of common sense.

The above represents my views on the way in which a foreign language should be approached. I have submitted what I regard as more than a *prima facie* case for taking into careful consideration certain facts that must be patent to all who have given any thought to the matter under discussion.

Having learned successfully—I venture to say—two foreign languages, by means of what I call the natural language-learning forces or powers or capacities inherent in us all, I feel in a position to suggest to you in the light of my personal experience—an experience shared by countless others—that you should so design your language courses that full account is taken of these forces.

I propose to send my two sons to your institute in order that one of them may learn French and the other German. In either case I would request that you should afford them the fullest opportunities of hearing the language spoken, of hearing it spoken in conditions that will enable them to associate the words with the things that these words stand for, and that you should instruct their teachers to use in the classroom no other language than the one studied—*until the pupils are able effectively to think in the foreign language.* I would request you to withhold from them all those things that weaken their natural powers of language absorption, and to administer to them in strong doses all those exercises and drills that give full scope to these powers. Teach them French or German through French or German. Exercise a strict discipline in these respects; ignore their possible requests for explanations in English; make no concessions to their possible complaints or lamentations; pay no attention to their bewilderment when faced with the difficulty of the French conjugation or the German declension.

Put them through the mill with a firm hand; instil into their minds the need for a severe linguistic discipline, affording them none of the short cuts that, in the experience of most, if not all, language-learners, prove to be the longest way round.

Comments on Letter 10

Our correspondent has not used the term 'as speech', but his attitude towards language-learning and teaching is one which coincides almost exactly with the interpretation of the term 'English, French, etc.', given in Part 1, Letter 6. In a sense, the one supplements the other, for if a language were not the thing you think *with* (and the writer of Letter 6 maintained that it was), then the claim by our correspondent here that real success in the acquirement of a language—native or foreign, first or second, third or fourth, fifth or sixth—is only attained by processes which enable the learner to think *in* the language being learned (and the difference of preposition does not imply a difference of meaning)— then this claim, we say, would be absolutely groundless.

Having decided that Letter 6 expressed the essential nature of a language, we shall have no difficulty in providing for our present correspondent's sons in the normal programme which is outlined in Part 3, without any modification at all.

LETTER 11. A FUNDAMENTAL FORMULA

You have invited me as a prospective student of your institute to ask myself and to tell you what I really mean when I say I want to learn Hungarian, how I would have you teach me it, and to which of the linguistic disciplines known to me I would be willing to submit myself. I welcome the opportunity you have given me to express myself on the subject.

For the last twenty-five years I have been lecturing and writing on linguistic methodology. I have never given my allegiance to any one particular school or doctrine, but have rather examined with fair thoroughness (and often tested in actual practice as a teacher or as a learner) each scheme or plan that has ever seemed to me to be of value. I have followed up with interest most of the controversies that have arisen (at various times and in various countries) in connexion with problems of the language classroom, from the time of Viëtor's manifesto (*Die Sprachunterricht muss umkehren*) down to the Coleman Report.[1] Moreover, I have had much experience in the classroom and as member of examining boards. If I preface my answer by such personal details it is not from any sense of vainglory, but as an indication that this answer of mine is likely to be of more weight than those that you may be receiving from people whose only claim to a hearing is that they intend to follow a language course at your institute.

What I have said so far may have given you the impression that I am going to treat you to a lengthy dissertation on linguistic methodology, that I shall proceed to a technical analysis of the contributions made to the subject by Sweet, Passy, Walther, Viëtor, Jespersen, Berlitz, Gouin, Sapir, Bloomfield, Cummings, de Sauzé, Coleman, Handschin, West, and so on, and that I shall sum them up and draw conclusions. I shall do nothing of the sort. On the contrary, I shall be exceedingly brief—the value of my communication, indeed, should consist in the fact that I shall say so much in so few words.

When we survey the immense field of linguistic pedagogy we are bewildered at its extent, its varied aspects, its complexity. Indeed, it is difficult to survey it as a whole. Its *facies* change according to the angle from which we survey it. Look at it from the angle of the phoneticians, and it appears a something with phonetics prominently in the foreground. From the angle of the grammarians, it seems centred about conjugation, declension, and syntax. From the angle of text-simplifiers and organizers of word-counts it seems based on lexicological statistics. From the angle of the 'direct reading' advocates it looks like a solid mass of reading matter surrounded vaguely by nebulosities called sounds, auditory images, paradigms, phonetic symbols, and conversational formulas. Look at it from any particular angle, and the general field of linguistic phenomena seems different and of a different nature. In the fable of the two knights and the shield one knight declared the shield to be of silver and the other maintained it to be of gold—the result was a combat. But, instead of looking at the present subject of debate from merely two different angles, the champions of this or that different school of linguistic pedagogy look at it respectively from dozens of angles—the result is a complication of controversies.

And yet, if we only know where to look, we can see clearly one outstanding fact in the midst of this many-sided mass of linguistic phenomena. From whatever angle we view the tangle of facts and fancies associated

[1] *The Teaching of Modern Foreign Languages in the United States*, by Algernon Coleman.

with the language-teaching problem we see this one fact constant and unchanging; and because it is constant and unchanging, it constitutes the centre, the very nucleus, the core itself, of the mass of linguistic phenomena—and it is the one and only fact that has the same appearance when viewed from any angle. And this fact is so simple that it can be reduced to a seven-word formula. It is the answer to the question, What is in its essence the process of learning a language? It is this: *Fusing linguistic symbols to the things symbolized.*

That is the beginning, the middle, and the end of the whole process of language-learning, in any and all conditions and circumstances. Interpret this formula aright—and you have the whole secret of successful language-study.

To fuse means, here, to form a perfect mental association or bond between two things, so that either brings the other to consciousness—as when the word 'telephone' brings to the mind of an English-speaking person the thing called a telephone, or as when the sentence 'Just pass me that book, will you?' brings to the mind of the English-speaking hearer or reader the notion of an informal request for the passing of a book. I am using the term 'fuse' because it is stronger than 'associate' or 'form a link'.

A *linguistic symbol* means here any word, semantic variety of that word, collocation of words, construction-pattern—in short, any linguistic device to symbolize something.[1]

The *thing symbolized* means here any conceivable thing for which a linguistic symbol stands, such as an object, an action, a quality, a relation, an attitude, etc., which it is the function of language to symbolize.

Here is a language of which you are completely ignorant; this means that not one of the linguistic symbols contained in it has become, in your mind, fused to the thing that it symbolizes. Here is a language that you *do* know; this means that a sufficient number of the linguistic symbols contained in it have become fused in your mind to the things they symbolize to enable you to use that language.

All classroom (or other) procedures that cause students to fuse linguistic symbols to what is symbolized by them are sound and economical procedures. All procedures that, while not directly causing students to effect such fusion, nevertheless serve as effective aids to subsequent fusion are also sound and economical procedures. All

---

[1] See the classified list in the Appendix of the various types of linguistic symbols.

procedures that do not in any way cause or help students to effect such fusions are unsound and uneconomical. In short, a procedure is sound and economical or unsound and uneconomical in the degree that it causes or helps or does not cause or help students to fuse linguistic symbols to the things they symbolize.

How do I want to learn Hungarian, you ask me. I answer, I want to learn it in such a way that I fuse in the shortest time the greatest number of useful Hungarian linguistic symbols to the things they symbolize. How would I have you teach me it, you ask. I answer, I would have you teach me it in such a way as to give me the greatest measure of aid in my work of fusion. To which linguistic disciplines known to me would I be willing to submit myself, you ask. I answer, I will submit to any linguistic disciplines that will enable me to effect these fusions with ease, rapidity, effectiveness, and interest.

Comments on Letter 11

From no other of the contributors to our symposium have we received an answer so clear and unassailable, and in its essence so concise as this one. Its writer seems to have singled out and wrested from that maze of confusing and baffling data the one fact that underlies all other facts connected with the learning or teaching of languages. He has stated this fact simply, and in such a way that none can deny it or underrate its importance. The essence of language-learning is the forming of bonds between the symbols of which a language is made up and the concepts or notions or thoughts for which they stand; that is what our correspondent states with emphasis and truth.

Having said this, it might be pointed out that in his insistence on the importance of what he describes as 'fusion' he has perhaps overlooked that there is one preliminary step to fusion which no language teacher can possibly afford to disregard. It is the process of what might be called 'identification'. Before we can fuse an unknown symbol to what is symbolized by it we have to come to know what it actually does symbolize. There is the sort of direct identification which consists in ascertaining that such and such a symbol stands invariably for such and such a thing symbolized; there is the sort of identification which consists in understanding the circumstances in which a known symbol is to be employed; and there is the sort of identification which consists in grasping the circumstances in which this rather than that known symbol is to be employed.

It is not that fusion is invariably preceded by identification. At times the two processes are simultaneous; at others a partial fusion may precede complete identification.

Now nobody can dispute the importance of this process of identification. It is the first part of learning symbols; it is so important, indeed, that up to the present much of the language-teaching the world over has taken the form of helping learners to identify. 'Book means *livre*', said the old-time teacher, or, a little later, his direct-method successor said only, 'Book', the while brandishing a volume. But the process in both cases was one of identification.

Our correspondent here with his emphasis on fusion has rendered an important service to an understanding of the processes of language-learning. The identification, which he has overlooked, is not without importance, but the fusion, which up to now has been fairly generally overlooked, is of much greater importance.

Finally, there is no valid reason why the process of identification should not be assisted by the use of the mother-tongue, except in the initial stages, where it is of the utmost importance to train the learner to develop the 'as speech' attitude, which results not only in a proficiency in the more natural and spontaneous types of identification, but also in the development of an almost unconscious fusing habit.

In connexion with this fusion there is probably another point which our correspondent has overlooked. This is to set down with any reasonable degree of detail the processes to be employed for the purpose of fusion. Possibly one of the most important of these is what the senior partner in this association has called 'catenizing'. This term serves to designate primarily that sort of memorizing that consists in becoming proficient in executing any succession of muscular movements automatically. The piano-player who can execute a passage without hesitation or without looking at the musical score is said to have catenized that passage. The actor who is word perfect has catenized all his lines. In the same way, the language-learner cannot be said to have catenized any succession of articulatory muscular movements until he can utter the linguistic unit in its entirety without hesitation or any process of piecing together. In other terms, catenizing is synonymous with mechanical memorizing.

But a preliminary process to this automatic succession of muscular movements may well be, and often is, one of the succession as an integral unit. Let us consider the succession of articulatory muscular movements associated with the unit *Il ne manquerait plus que cela*. It will be admitted that this is a linguistic unit that has to be learned as a whole, and not built up from its component parts. The first aim will obviously be to cause the learner so to recognize it; the second to reproduce it. It may be that the two phases of the process will be simultaneous, or it may be that the recognition capacity will precede the production capacity. But however this may be, the fundamental training in catenizing has to be given. Which amounts to saying to the learner: 'This has got to be taken in as one thing, in order that ultimately it may be given out as one thing.'

We have spoken of catenizing in relation to what has been called in another connexion 'long spans'. And we have done so because in this connexion the need of such catenizing is immediately obvious. We would, however, point out that the initial process of all fusing, whether it be of what is called a 'word' or any other unit, is one of catenizing.

The first phase of the process of fusing *livre* to that composite mass of cardboard, paper, and stitches is the catenization, the learning by heart, the capacity to articulate spontaneously the sounds which go to make up the word *livre*.

It thus emerges from what has gone before that the essential processes of language-learning are *identification* and then *fusion*, this latter involving necessarily the catenizing activity.

From such clearly stated premises as these all may draw their conclusions, and if these conclusions are not all in agreement the starting-point at least is the same (and this is a progress in the history of linguistic pedagogy). Rightly or wrongly, some conclude that the 100 per cent direct method plan is the surest and the most economical for aiding fusion. Rightly or wrongly, the exponents of the oral method state that it is the oral-aural approach that leads most effectively to the fusing of symbol and symbolized. Rightly or wrongly, others claim that the visual approach or the motor-graphic approach is more or equally effective. Rightly or wrongly, some consider that a preliminary grounding in grammar, phonetics, or semantics serves as an aid to the subsequent process of fusion. Rightly or wrongly, Dr Michael West in India or Professor Otto F. Bond in Chicago may testify that the reading-skill is of primary importance in India or America, and that therefore the written symbol, above all, is to be fused to what it symbolizes. Rightly or wrongly, Bovée in Chicago and some of us in Tokyo believe that the natural and spontaneous bond is that between the acoustic-articulatory image and the notion (and that if the image is actually phonated the bond is all the stronger). Rightly or wrongly, the statistical lexicologists suggest selected vocabularies and simplified texts, so that the number of bonds may be lessened. Rightly or wrongly, Mr C. K. Ogden with his Basic English proposes boldly to reduce the number of English linguistic symbols to 850, so that this number of fusions may suffice for the purposes of a universal auxiliary language. (It is true that these 850 symbols include nothing except just ordinary words or 'monologemes', irrespective of their semantic varieties and the non-normal collocations and construction-patterns into which they enter.) Rightly or wrongly, the IALA (International Auxiliary Language Association) people are endeavouring to ascertain the nature of linguistic symbols and to catalogue the things they symbolize. (Mr Ogden and his orthologists, by the way, are doing the same thing.) Rightly or wrongly, 'the great ideomologist' Saito of Japan, spent his life in working out the relations between English linguistic symbols and the things they symbolize—incidentally discovering which were the most exactly corresponding Japanese linguistic symbols.

Looking round where we may, we note that all interested in the field of learning or teaching of languages (be it the mother-tongue or some foreign-language) are basing their research and efforts on the fundamental dictum formulated by our correspondent. One of the contributors to our symposium speaks of the linguistic powers with which we are endowed by nature—he means the powers of fusing linguistic symbols to the things they symbolize. He speaks of the respective mental linguistic processes of French Alphonse and English Johnny, and compares them with those of Robinson Crusoe's Man Friday—again he means those processes by which we are enabled to fuse symbol and thing symbolized.

We welcome our correspondent as a student of Hungarian in our institute—and still more as head of the English Department of the institute, for he has been good enough to accept this post, which we offered him as the result of having read his contribution to our symposium.

GENERAL COMMENTS ON PART 2

So many men, so many attitudes—ranging from the most classical to the most utilitarian, from the most trustful to the most opinionated, from the most general to the most particular! These attitudes do not, with a few notable exceptions, represent the views of people who are familiar with the problems of language-teaching, or, indeed, with the problems of teaching anything, but they are views with which every language teacher must make himself familiar if only for the purpose of demonstrating their inaccuracy.

Without thinking that these attitudes are in any sense the right ones language teachers must, however, take them into consideration when planning courses of study in order to see, first, how many of them can profitably be utilized, and, secondly, how many of them lie outside the sphere of the language-learning business altogether. Expressed more bluntly, the problem is something like this: the man who wants to learn a language knows pretty definitely what sort of mastery of the language he wishes to attain, and in almost all cases he thinks he knows how he should attain it. We have to listen very carefully to the first part of his explanation and to accept without question the decision he has made. When a man says, 'I want to be able to make myself understood among the natives of France', it is pointless for us to say to him, 'You ought to want to be able to read Corneille.' Perhaps he ought, but that's between him and his conscience: it's no business of ours. It may be, of course, that his requirements are such that meeting them cannot possibly be fitted into a general language course at all, and if this is the case it is our duty to tell him so, and to make special arrangements for him if possible, or to bid him a regretful but firm good-day. By no means must we let those of his requirements which do not come into the sphere of language-learning in any general sense influence us in the planning of our course, for if we do so he will not get what he wants—which is regrettable—and neither will the majority of our students—which is infinitely more regrettable. As an illustration of this point let us take the case of the writer of Letter 2 in Part 2. He does not want to learn a language, but wants to make further research in the problems of general phonetics. It is our duty to explain to him that, although phonetics is an important aid to language-learning, it is not language-learning in itself; and therefore, although his aim is legitimate, it cannot be catered for in a language course—or, rather, if it *is* so catered for the language course will suffer. The trouble is, however, that anybody who wants to do anything with, about, through, in, or on a language makes a clean sweep of all these important prepositions and says he wants to learn 'English' or 'French', etc., while language teachers endeavour for the most part to reconcile all these claims and succeed in producing the pseudo-scientific muddle which is the average language course in any seat of learning today.

But the attitude of the writer of the final contribution to Part 2 of this book is the one that puts him into a special category. We listened with patience to some of our contributors, with a certain measure of impatience to others, with pleasure and interest to still others, but we read with an unfeigned enthusiasm the one who diagnosed language-learning to be nothing other than fusing symbols to the things they symbolize. It is he, more than any of the others, who has given us the keynote of our policy and of the procedures and disciplines that we shall urge or impose on our students.

'With an unfeigned enthusiasm', we have said. We are mindful that in the dry schools of pedagogy enthusiasm is discounted and the enthusiast is a suspect—he is probably a doctrinaire or a crank. Nevertheless, we are not ashamed here to be enthusiastic, for we are convinced that the writer of the final contribution has got nearer than have any of his fellow-contributors to the centre or nucleus of all that concerns this language-learning business. His concisely expressed findings accord with those of the contributor who voiced the creed of Dr Rouse, formerly of the Perse School, Cambridge, of the contributor who claimed that the 'as speech' attitude was the right one, and of the contributor who invoked the linguistic powers with which we are endowed by nature. If the findings of many who have made an almost lifelong study of the problems facing us (notwithstanding the adverse findings of those whose experience has been more localized, more special, or more superficial), corroborated by personal experience in many fields and in many places, have brought conviction to us—conviction and therefore certainty, and therefore relief from hesitation, perplexity, and doubt—there is every reason for us to add to our cold judgment some measure of warm enthusiasm.

3 Business: an outline of a comprehensive language course

INTRODUCTORY

On the basis of the foregoing matter we hereby set out our conception of an ideal language course. Linguistic ideals, like all others, are guided by a dual consideration of principle and expediency. In devising our programme we, too, shall be guided by this dual consideration, and shall first set down the general principles governing our course, from which neither we nor our pupils shall deviate, and then we shall make a detailed statement as to the practical application of those principles. The detailed programme is—in our considered opinion—likely to be of use to, and to produce effective results for, a large majority of language-learners the world over.

This programme as it stands will necessarily be subject to considerable modifications to meet the various needs of students of divergent race, age, aptitude, and degree of accord with, or resistance to, disciplines; also the varying sizes of classes, periods over which the lessons are spread, etc. Considerable modifications also will be required, depending upon the existence or non-existence, in the language to be taught, of an irrational and unphonetic spelling system (as in English), of a complicated grammar system (as in Russian), and of an unfamiliar writing system (as in Japanese) for all Western peoples, and vice versa.

Principles

(1) The course is designed on the basic principle that the student shall be caused from the very first lesson not merely to identify the unfamiliar linguistic symbols, but also to fuse them to the things they symbolize. By so doing he will come to regard the language he is learning as a new instrument of thought—that is, 'as speech'. This means that throughout his instruction he is to be discouraged from making use of his mother-tongue *for any purpose connected with fusion*.

(2) We do not denounce the use of the student's mother-tongue for purposes other than what we have called fusion. As one of our correspondents[1] pointed out, by some means or other we have to bridge the gulf between the linguistic capacity of the native child at the age of two and that of the foreign person at whatever age he takes up his studies. We are convinced that this gulf may be bridged by certain procedures which, though 'unnatural', are nevertheless effective and helpful. The first of these is the teaching of phonetic theory in the initial stages to secure from the outset that accuracy of pronunciation without which the 'as speech' attitude is extremely difficult to acquire. This instruction can only be effectively given in the student's native language, and must be so given.

The second aid in bridging the gulf is that procedure which codifies the language for the more mature mind of a foreign learner, and thus enables him to employ the material presented to him with greater accuracy and precision. These explanations will be given only in so far as they are codifications to assist use, but when they are given they will be given in the language with which the student is most familiar. The reason for this must be obvious: these explanations will be rare, but of rare value, and therefore it is essential that there should not be the faintest misunderstanding or incompleteness of understanding of their import.

(3) Although we believe that occasionally and in special circumstances it is not only permissible but positively helpful to answer such questions as 'Why is this construction used, and not that other construction?' we adopt as a general principle that we are teaching *what* is said, *which* is said, and *when* and *where* it is said, in the foreign language, rather than *why* it is said. In other words, we are reducing to a minimum information *about* the language, because information *about* the language is contrary to the 'as speech' attitude. But when we have said that we are reducing our answers to the question *why* to a minimum we have to explain, at any rate in general terms, what that minimum is. We will not answer the *why* that merely stimulates irrelevant thought, but we will answer the *why* that stimulates action, linguistic action— that is, use of the language. The pupil asks, 'Why must we say in German, '*Ich schribe mit der Kreide*', instead of '*mit die Kreide*'?' The answer (a perfectly legitimate answer to a legitimate question) is, 'Because the preposition *mit* is invariably followed by the dative.' It is more than a legitimate answer to a question. It is a piece of

[1] In Part 2, Letter 10.

comprehensive information which should be given even before the
question is asked. It is like telling a man in a strange town that all
main roads going south lead to the river. If he knows what a main
road is and knows the lie of the town he can get to the river from any
part of the town—and that's what we want him to do. If the same man
asked us *why* the main roads going south lead to the river we should
suppose that he didn't want to know his way about the town at all,
but something about the psychology of the town-planners or about the
nature of the soil in the neighbourhood. And we should refuse to give
the information even if we knew it, deeming it to be useless for his
purpose and wasteful of our time. If our student of German asks us,
'Why is the preposition *mit* invariably followed by the dative?' we shall,
for these same reasons, refuse to answer him. We shall refuse to give
information which is useless for the purpose of the language-learner,
and not only wasteful of our time, but of his too. The last word has not
been said on this subject. We have declared our willingness to give
classified information which shall be relevant and helpful, but all
classified relevant information is not necessarily helpful—usually
because the information is inaccurate, or because no accurate classification is possible, or because no classification is really helpful in the
circumstances.

(4) The student will be taught to read the foreign language by the
same processes as those by which he was taught to read his first language. In the same way that he was not called upon to read those
words of his mother-tongue which he did not already possess as speech,
so now he will not be called upon to read those foreign words that he
does not already possess as speech. In this way the vicious process
known as 'deciphering' (i.e. worrying out the pronunciation and
meaning of words presented in their spelling-form) will be avoided. In
other terms, he shall not be allowed to form a visual graphic image of
a word until he has come to possess its image acoustically. We stress
this because we are convinced that to allow so-called visual images of
foreign words is tantamount to allowing translation, and this, as we
have said under the heading Principle (1), we are determined to pro-
hibit. If the pupil sees an unfamiliar word (i.e. a word of which he is
not acoustically conscious) he forms of it an acoustic image without any
doubt, but it partakes of the nature of an acoustic descriptive paraphrase in his own tongue. If he reads *manquer* without having assimilated
it acoustically in relation to a familiar context his acoustic image of it
is something of this kind: that thing spelt m-a-n-q-u-e-r, with a sort

of 'lacking-missing' meaning. Now we maintain that a man who ought to be thinking simply *manquer*, but is thinking in the terms described above, is thinking in a muddle—a muddle which will hold up his linguistic development considerably. In other terms, the student will be taught to read linguistic symbols that have already become, in his mind, fused to the things symbolized.

THE PRACTICAL APPLICATION OF THE PRINCIPLES

Stage 1. Specific Lessons in Pronunciation—Free Auditory Assimilation (Of a duration of, let us say, 30 hours)

(a) SPECIFIC LESSONS IN PRONUNCIATION

Probably the chief cause of that almost universal linguistic disease, a bad (or relatively bad) pronunciation, is that students are caused to speak the foreign language before they have had adequate opportunities for observing or for imitating the phonetic phenomena of the foreign language. The actual difficulties of acquiring a passable pronunciation are largely illusory. Given a fair chance of hearing and imitating the sounds, either isolated or as successions—as 'slices of sonority'—the willing student rarely fails to give a good account of himself in all that concerns pronunciation. The traditional difficulty of the English *th*, of the French *u*, of the Spanish *ll*, and of the German *ch* can be explained by the fact that the willing student has not received ample opportunities for hearing these sounds or for imitating them, coupled with the fact that his teacher does not know the physiological basis of them.

At the outset, then, we give our pupils ample opportunities for observing, imitating, and understanding the physiological basis of the phonetic units of the language that they are learning. We are aided by phonetic symbols, by diagrams, by charts, by the resources of experimental phonetics—and, above all, by the resources dictated by common sense. If the English student of French (misled by his associations connected with the form of the letter *u*) imagines that the French *u* is a variation of the English *u* as in the word 'use', we, with the resources of normative phonetics behind us, show him that in reality this French *u* is like the English *ee* of 'see' plus lip-rounding. Aided by these same resources, we demonstrate to our pupils that English *th* is not a *t* plus *h*, but a breath between teeth plus tongue-blade.

Our specific exercises in pronunciation take more than one form. One of the forms is what is called 'ear-training'. The teacher articulates something once or several times. What was it that the students heard? 'Was it this?' (a phonetic symbol written on the blackboard). 'Or was it this?' (another symbol written on the blackboard). Or, alternatively, 'Did you hear me say the vowel of "bold"? If so, raise your hands. (Hands up please!)', or 'Did you hear me say the vowel of "bald"? (Hands up please!)'. Or, again, 'Write down in phonetic symbols exactly what you think I pronounced'. (This is called phonetic dictation.)

Our specific exercises may take another form—for instance, 'systematic articulation exercises.' The teacher will say to the students, 'Listen; listen carefully. Reproduce what you hear—or what you think you hear. Imitate me. Make just the same sound (or succession of sounds) as I make. Be a parrot or a gramophone recording instrument. Don't translate my sounds into the sounds of your own language. Don't think of spelling. Don't think of your own language. Just reproduce. Make the same noises as I am making. Think of noises and not of letters. You, an English (or Polish) student of French, hear me say, [aksebo]. Say the same thing, [aksebo], without reference to *Ah, que c'est beau!*—which is the conventional spelling representation in French orthography of what English people would express by "Isn't that lovely"?'

By these and other procedures we cause our pupils to listen to the foreign language and to enunciate it in the manner of the native listener and speaker. Give the student of the foreign language a chance—a reasonable chance—and he will react to it. Withhold from him that chance—and don't blame him if he fails.

The giving of this chance is part of the business of the teacher of the foreign language during the first thirty hours of his teaching. During this first thirty hours he can secure much of what he wishes to secure in the matter of pronunciation.

In the institute that we have in mind every one of our teachers will, as a matter of course, possess in an adequate measure the pronunciation of the language that he is teaching.

(b) FREE AUDITORY ASSIMILATION

It is in Stage 1, then, that the students are given intensive and systematic exercises in pronunciation, these including ear-training exercises and exercises in articulation.

It is undesirable that pupils should be allowed to answer questions or even to speak in any way (*a*) before they are thoroughly familiar with the sounds of the language and how to produce them, and (*b*) before they have had adequate opportunities for hearing the language spoken more or less continuously while associating it with its meaning.

As we have said, it is in Stage 1 that the students are made familiar with the sounds of the language and how to produce them. It will also be in Stage 1 that the students will be given adequate opportunities for hearing the language spoken more or less continuously while associating it with its meaning.

The simplest and most natural way of so causing the pupils to hear the language spoken is for the teacher to talk to them continuously, illustrating each sentence by appropriate gestures and actions. The pupils listen and watch; and by dint of listening and watching they come to understand the general meaning of what is said by the teacher. In the first instance this understanding will be of a very diffused nature; they will grasp the meaning vaguely, and loose associations will be set up between the words they hear and the gestures which accompany them. As time goes on the understanding will become more precise and less diffused, and the attention will be more focused on the individual words and intimate word-groups.

Example 1. The teacher holds up a book and says, 'Book' (or 'A book' or 'This is a book'); he holds up a pencil and says, 'Pencil' (or 'A pencil' or 'This is a pencil'). The pupils perceive the words 'book' and 'pencil' and associate (or tend to associate) the words with the objects for which they stand.

Example 2. The teacher holds up or points to a red book, a red pencil, a red ball, saying, 'This book (pencil, ball) is red', or 'This is a red book (pencil, ball)'. Then he contrasts the red book with a blue book, the red pencil with a yellow pencil, the red ball with a white ball, etc., saying, 'This book's red'; 'This pencil's yellow'; 'This ball's red'; 'This ball's white'. Or, 'This is a red book'; 'This is a blue book', etc. The pupils perceive the words 'red', 'blue', 'yellow', 'white', and associate (or tend to associate) these words with the colours for which they stand. They also come to perceive the incidental words 'this', 'is', 'a', and note the order of the words in the sentence.

Example 3. The teacher puts a book on the desk, a pencil on a chair, and a box on the floor. He says 'This is a book', 'This is a desk', 'The book's on the desk', 'This is a pencil', 'This is a chair', 'The pencil's on the chair', etc., etc. He speaks of a match being *on* a box, *in* a box, *in front of* a box, *behind* a box, accompanying each statement by an appropriate gesture. The pupils come to understand the meanings of the prepositions and of the various sentences.

Example 4. The teacher slowly opens a book, a box, the door, the window, and says, 'I'm opening the book', 'I'm opening the box', etc. Then he contrasts opening with shutting. He goes to the door, to the window, to the desk, and says, 'I'm going to the door', etc. He contrasts going with coming, standing up with sitting down, pushing with pulling, etc. The pupils perceive the words and the actions to which they correspond, and tend to remember the words, and to associate them with their meanings; they will recognize the words when they hear them again.

Example 5. The teacher touches the desk, the floor, his shoulder, the blackboard, and says, 'I'm touching the desk', etc. He tries to touch the top of the blackboard, the ceiling, or some other object beyond his reach, and failing to do so, says, 'I can't touch the top of the black-board', etc. He contrasts 'I can' with 'I can't'. He tells his pupils what they can or cannot touch, lift, read, etc. The pupils perceive the words 'can' and 'can't' and associate them with the ideas to which they correspond.

In the foregoing description and examples of free auditory assimi-lation we see that the pupil has nothing to do except to sit, listen, and associate the things he hears with their meanings. In a slightly more developed variety of free auditory assimilation he is called upon to react, and by reacting not only to demonstrate his understanding, but also to participate more actively in the proceedings. But it is still too early for his reactions to be articulatory: they take the form of execut-ing certain orders given by the teacher. It is obvious that this is a close approximation to the processes by which the native language was acquired.

The teacher tells the pupil in the foreign language to perform some action; the pupil, understanding the words of the command or the gesture that accompanies it, performs the action. If the teacher has reason to suppose that the pupil will not understand the command he may as a preliminary demonstrate the meaning of one or more of the words contained in it.

Example 1. The teacher points to various objects, saying, 'This is a desk', 'This is the blackboard', 'This is the floor', 'This is my head', etc. He then touches these various objects, saying, 'I'm touching the desk'. 'I'm touching the blackboard', etc. He then issues the commands, 'Touch your desk', 'Touch the floor', 'Touch your head', etc. The pupil, having come to understand the meaning of 'desk', blackboard', 'head', 'touch', etc., executes the commands.

Example 2. The teacher, believing that his pupil will react successfully even if he has received no preliminary drilling in the meanings of the words, says to the pupil (with or without gesture), 'Touch the floor'. The pupil executes the command.

Example 3. The teacher, with or without preliminary demonstration or gesture, says to the pupil, 'Open your book, turn to page twenty-eight, and show it to me'. The pupil does so.

The commands may be given to one pupil at a time or to the whole class.

Stage 2. Lessons in Speaking (Of a duration of, let us say, 30 hours)

Stage 1 is, as we have seen, the pre-speaking stage; Stage 3 is, as we shall see, the stage marking the introduction of reading and writing; Stage 2 is the one in which the pupils are taught to speak. In the same way as the capacity to recognize and reproduce accurately the foreign sounds, plus a certain capacity in understanding the foreign language when spoken, has prepared the pupils for speaking themselves, so the capacity to speak gained in this stage will prepare them for the study in Stage 3 of the language as written. Again, it might be pointed out that we are following the so-called natural processes. There is a period of speaking training which precedes training in reading, and capacity in the first is undoubtedly an aid to acquirement of the second.

We have put this period at thirty hours; this we consider a good average period, but the number of hours is by no means immutable. Where the writing system of the language to be learned approximates to phonetic regularity (as, for example, in German), or where the writing system is entirely divorced from sound associations so far as the pupils are concerned (as in the case of Chinese), this period will be considerably shorter or may even be omitted altogether.

In the case of a language phonetically irregular, but using the same alphabet as the learner's own (as in the case of English for French students and vice versa), reading and conventional orthography should be withheld for an even longer period.

As to the form which this training shall take, we would suggest the procedures coming under the general title of Conventional Question-and-Answer Work.

Conventional question-and-answer work is the most effective of all the language-learning exercises ever devised. In its various forms and grades it initiates, develops, and utilizes the natural language-learning forces with which we are all endowed. It is the quickest and most effective approach both to the spoken and to the written aspects of the language; it is the shortest cut to reading; and it may be adapted for purposes so diverse as the teaching of conversation, of abstract grammar, of composition, and of pronunciation.

The essential point of the procedure is this: the teacher asks a question in the foreign language;[1] the pupil, *borrowing most of or all the material contained in the question*, answers it.

The question must be of such a nature that it admits of the following:

(*a*) An obvious answer, not an answer that requires one or more complicated acts of judgment, memory, or appreciation, or one requiring data unknown to the pupil.

(*b*) An easy answer, not one that requires the use of words unknown to the student, or (in the earlier stages) of too many words not occurring in the question.

(*c*) An answer which is *to the point*—that is, precisely that answer which is required by that particular question.

The pupil hears and understands the question, and answers it immediately. The linguistic contents of the question (words, form, etc.) are such that they are immediately associated, not with any words or forms of the mother-tongue, but with the thing, the idea, the concept, for which they stand. The less, also, the linguistic contents are associated with the visual image of any written form, the more effective will the teaching value of the procedure be.

The student, with the words of the question still echoing in his ears, adapts or converts them into the appropriate answer. He utilizes the linguistic contents of the question, and embodies them so far as possible in his answer. He selects that part of the question which will serve as the answer, or by simple substitution, conversion, or completion, modifies the question so that it will serve as the answer.

Putting it simply, the words used by the teacher in his question pass inward through the student's ear, and a moment later, slightly or considerably modified, pass outward through his vocal organs.

Let us recapitulate the above by giving a concrete instance of the nature of the stimulus and of the reaction.

---

[1] After the pupils have been well trained in this technique the teacher may at his discretion call upon his best pupils to ask the questions.

THE TEACHER ASKS A QUESTION; let us say, 'Is an elephant a large or a small animal?'

(*a*) the question admits of an obvious answer. (*b*) The question admits of an easy answer, for we must assume the linguistic contents to be known to the student; moreover, all the words except one (it) are contained in the question. (*c*) The question admits of an answer to the point; there is one, and only one, perfect answer to the question.

THE LEARNER HEARS AND UNDERSTANDS THE QUESTION.

The form, 'Is a [noun] a [adjective] or a [adjective] [noun]?' as well as the words, 'elephant', 'large', 'small', and 'animal', are known to the learner.

The student, with the words of the question still ringing in his ears, adapts them by omission, conversion, and substitution in the following way: 'It's a large animal'. 'Or a small' has been omitted, 'is' has been converted to ' 's ', and 'it' has been substituted for 'an elephant'.

The chief indication that this is the right way of utilizing the procedure should be clear.

The learner is forced to observe the words and the form of the question, to observe the sounds, the succession of sounds, the choice of words, the word-order, etc. By thus being forced to observe he forms, develops, and uses the habit of *auditory observation*.

Having observed correctly, he finds that the easiest way to frame his answer is to *reproduce* a large part of the question. By so doing he forms, develops, and uses the habit of *oral imitation*.

By hearing and repeating constantly the same construction-patterns and word groups he forms the habit of fluent and accurate delivery.

The learner comes to recognize that it is easier to answer the question while the words and forms contained in it are still in his ears; he comes to recognize that if he performs any act of mental translation he will lose the benefit of the acoustic image, of the echo (or positive after-image) of the words he has heard. Consequently he tends not to translate mentally, and by thus avoiding the words of his mother-tongue he comes to associate more and more the linguistic content with its semantic content; in other words, he tends to fuse the words and forms to what they symbolize—another valuable speech-learning habit.

The answer requires a certain modification of the question; words are omitted; pronouns are substituted for nouns; various words are substituted for 'what', 'who', 'which', 'where', 'when', 'how', etc.; and various words are converted into another form. All such acts are closely connected with that speech-learning habit called *composition by analogy*.

In short, the chief reason why the procedure as here interpreted is the right one is that it does encourage, even compel, the learner to form, develop, and use the three most essential speech-learning habits.

Let us now contrast this manner of interpreting and carrying out the question-and-answer procedure with one that tends to give negative results or that may, indeed, positively encourage bad habits of language-learning.

In the first place, the teacher may ask a question of such a nature that it admits of no *obvious* answer. The reply may require one or more complicated acts of judgment, memory, or appreciation, or it may require data unknown to the learner. On one or other of these grounds we must consider as more or less unsuitable such questions as:

Which is worse for the health: to eat too much or to eat too little?

In what year did King George V come to the throne?

How much is 242 multiplied by 9?

Which is more beautiful: vocal music or instrumental music?

What is the capital of Bulgaria?

The teacher may ask a question of such a nature that it admits of no *easy* answer, because it would require either words unknown to the student or too many words not occurring in the question. On one or the other of these grounds we must consider as more or less unsuitable such questions as:

How did Columbus come to discover America?

What did Sir Isaac Newton do?

To what extent are we indebted to science?

What happened after that?

In these and in other ways the teacher may ask unsuitable questions, but such errors of method are insignificant when compared with the wrong ways in which the pupil is taught or encouraged to answer.

The usual tendency among pupils (more especially adult learners) is to translate the question into their mother-tongue, consider it and form the answer in the mother-tongue, and then translate it back into the foreign language.

We need hardly point out that such a procedure is worse than useless. It forms and utilizes not one of the natural language-learning forces. The pupil is encouraged and tempted to form and to utilize habits which are ineffective, or nearly so, for the purpose of mastering a foreign language.

Another wrong procedure is that by which—in answer to a question—the pupil recites a sentence from his text or, worse, actually reads the sentence from his text.

Thus we may sometimes hear such a dialogue as the following (if, indeed, we can call it a dialogue):

TEACHER. What did the King give the man?

PUPIL [*reciting or reading*]. 'The King was so pleased with this witty reply that he ordered a bag of gold to be given to the man.'

TEACHER. To whom did the King give the gold?

PUPIL [*reciting or reading*]. 'The King was so pleased with this witty reply that he ordered a bag of gold to be given to the man.'

TEACHER. Was the King pleased or not?

PUPIL [*reciting or reading*]. 'The King was so pleased,' etc., etc. (as before).

TEACHER. Why did the King give the man a bag of gold?

PUPIL [*reciting or reading*]. 'The King was so pleased,' etc., etc. (as before.

Stage 3. Lessons in Reading and Writing (Of a duration of, let us say, 30 hours)

It is in Stage 3 that we cause our pupils to learn to handle either the unfamiliar alphabet (for instance, the Russian alphabet for English students) or the unfamiliar uses to which the letters of a familiar alphabet are put (for instance, the French spelling system for English students).

We distinguish here between the two things: learning to handle the unfamilar alphabet or spelling system and learning to read in the full sense of the term—i.e. learning to make an immediate and accurate recognition of a succession of acoustic images from their written or printed symbols, together with a full understanding of the meaning.[1]

Again, we have set down thirty hours as a good average period. If, however, the alphabet is an unfamiliar one, and if the spelling system that it serves is an irregular one, this period may be too short. In the contrary case it may be too long. Much depends also upon the degree of proficiency attained by our pupils in the two preceding stages. One who has become perfectly familiar with the vocabulary so far presented (in point of form and meaning) will learn to use the unfamiliar alphabet or spelling system with greater ease—and hence greater speed—than

[1] Dr Michael West has admirably and succinctly defined reading as a 'process of sight-sound sense', adding that sound may be actual speech or merely auditory and kinaesthetic image.

one whose powers of retaining vocabulary are so weak that he has not been able to assimilate the material, or has assimilated it imperfectly.

As we have noted in discussing Principle (4), 'The student will be taught to read the foreign language by the same processes as those by which he was taught to read his first language'. The elementary reading texts put before him will contain none but familiar material. The procedure will be somewhat as follows:

Instead of the traditional method of first teaching the name of the letters from *a* to *z* or *alpha* to *omega*, we select some half-dozen letters (or syllabic symbols, as the case may be) of the most frequent occurrence and regular phonetic values and combine them into words familiar to the student, who learns them by the 'look-and-say' process. We add more letters and combine them into new words until the whole of the alphabet has become familiar both as isolated letters and in simple combinations.

When it comes to the actual reading of connected texts the teacher will first read out the first sentence; then the pupils will read it out in imitation of the model—first in chorus, then individually. The second and subsequent sentences will be read off in the same way. In the end the pupils will read out the whole of the text, partly by recognizing the shape of the words, partly by deducing the word from its spelling, partly by memory, and partly by guessing from the context what the word might be.

We are indebted to Dr L. Faucett, the author of *The Teaching of English in the Far East*,[1] for the device of teaching reading by 'flash-cards'. A number of strips of cardboard are prepared, each having printed on it a simple sentence cast in the form of a command or a question. In the initial stage, the showing of the slip accompanies the oral procedures described in Stages 1 and 2. Subsequently the slips are displayed without oral accompaniment, the pupils giving the appropriate response. At each repetition the slips are displayed for a shorter time until the pupils are able to take in what is printed on the slip as a single span and at a glance.

Stage 4. Lessons in the Remaining Major Mechanisms
Direct Method Composition Exercises (Of a duration of, let us say, 30 hours)
We find upon examination of any language that its main structure is made up, first of a limited number of extremely important and

[1] Harrap, 1927.

constantly occurring, and secondly, of an extremely large number of relatively unimportant and comparatively seldom occurring, symbols of a kind that suggest the title 'mechanisms'.[1]

Among the former we find in most languages the mechanisms for indicating, for instance, interrogation, possession, plurality, pastness, causative, potential, desiderative, conditional, etc. Among the latter we find those mechanisms not dignified with, and therefore presumably not worthy of, distinctive grammatical nomenclature, which express, for instance, intensity, reluctance, exclamatory emotional reaction, gratitude and its degrees, apology, indecision, modest disclaimers, and a desire to say as little as possible in as many words as possible.

Acquaintance with, and capacity to use, the major mechanisms are the *sine qua non* of linguistic attainment, and in recognition of this all language courses worthy of the name contain all or most of them. What those major mechanisms are for each individual language must be worked out by the textbook planner in each language. There is, of course, considerable variation. In both Spanish and English the difference between 'I write' and 'I am writing' is expressed explicitly by grammar mechanism; in French and German it is not. A teacher who teaches *en train de* plus the infinitive as a major French mechanism is robbing his pupils of time which might be given to what is a major mechanism in French and not in either Spanish or English—viz. the *on* construction. As a matter of fact, he is not teaching French in any real sense: he is teaching French in relation to other languages—one of the most fatal obstacles to the inculcation of the 'as speech' attitude.

The acquirement of these mechanisms constitutes the first important phase, as well as the phase of first importance, in language-learning. During this acquisition progress is measurable and grading is of the utmost importance; the pupil's linguistic career is made or marred in this period. Unfortunately the word 'elementary' has lost its vital force. If instead of 'elementary' we used 'fundamental' to describe this period and these processes we should in fact have said no more, but we should have conveyed immeasurably more.

We are now concerned with the last stage of the fundamental or elementary—call it what you will—period of language-learning, the period concerned with the teaching of the remaining major mechanisms.

At this juncture it may be appropriate to point out again that the programme that we are setting down is in the nature of an ordered succession of attainment. First the sound, rendering possible free

[1] For further amplification of this, see the Appendix.

auditory assimilation, which in its turn renders possible the use of spoken language, which, again in its turn, makes possible effective reading. Now the power of reading—together with its active complement, writing—is facilitating the acquirement of the remaining major mechanisms; and, as we shall see, the acquiring of the major mechanisms will constitute the fundamentals, the foundation on which the student may build whatever linguistic edifices he will—the airy castles of literature, the solid fortresses of philology, the utilitarian blocks of commercial correspondence, the bungalows or hotels (the latter often literally) of fluent colloquialism—or, like the majority of language-learners, nothing at all.

The procedures that we shall adopt for the teaching of the remaining major mechanisms are as follows.

The teaching will be based on graded reading texts, each one of which will provide one or more of these major mechanisms, together with a vocabulary, chosen partly in accordance with the findings of lexicological statistics, and partly according to the needs imposed by the mechanism that it is desired to teach.

Each of these reading texts will be preceded by an oral introduction, this for the most part taking the form of the now familiar procedures of free auditory assimilation and question-and-answer work. By these procedures the semantic value of all new words and the mechanism in connexion with which they are introduced will be demonstrated and drilled. These procedures, which were originally used as a means of forming speech-learning habits, will thus be utilized for a new purpose—viz. that of vocabulary extension.

At this point, in connexion with these reading texts, a new procedure will be introduced, one which has been made possible by the introduction of reading and writing—viz. direct method composition exercises.

What is the nature of these exercises? Before answering this question it would be better to explain their purpose. This is to supply the same stimuli to graded and accurate composition in the foreign language as have hitherto been furnished by translation exercises, without involving at this early stage processes so dangerous to the 'as speech' attitude. How are we to get our pupils to write the foreign language often, and at home, when we are not available to give oral stimuli? The answer of the majority of teachers is twofold. 'I can give free composition', they will say, 'but if I do so the pupils will use, or attempt to use, any sort of mechanism and any sort of vocabulary, and almost inevitably will resort to that sort of translation which has the least vestige of profit, that which consists of an attempt to reproduce word for word in the foreign language some complicated expression which has been thought and composed in the mother-tongue.' 'Let us be realists', say such teachers; 'free composition leads to super-pernicious translation—to translation at its worst; let us, rather, frankly call our exercises translation, and by so doing keep the work within the bounds of the pupil's knowledge of the foreign language.' Consequently, they recommend graded translation exercises, and if their modern colleagues or consciences reproach them they ask, 'What other way have we of getting written work done?' The answer is, 'There are eight other ways, which we shall now proceed to describe'.

(a) COMPOSITION THROUGH ANSWERS

The pupil is given a number of suitable questions in written form. He answers them by writing. Unlike those used for the purpose of 'conventional question-and-answer work', these questions generally require careful reflection on the part of the pupil, being more difficult and incidentally far less numerous.

(b) COMPOSITION BY CONVERSION

The pupil is given a number of sentences all of the same (or a very similar) type. Each sentence is 'converted' by the pupils into some other form designated by the teacher.

Example 1 : First to Third Person Singular

Original Sentence	Converted Sentence
Je vais à la gare.	Il va à la gare.
Je finis mon devoir.	Il finit son devoir.
Je comprends.	Il comprend.

Example 2 : Present to Past Indefinite

Original Sentence	Converted Sentence
Je vais à la gare.	Je suis allé(e) à la gare.
Je finis mon devoir.	J'ai fini mon devoir.
Je comprends.	J'ai compris.

Example 3 : Affirmative to Negative

Original Sentence	Converted Sentence
Je vais à la gare.	Je ne vais pas à la gare.
Je prends une leçon.	Je ne prends pas de leçon.
J'ai compris.	Je n'ai pas compris.

Example 4: Present to Future

The following passage is composed in the present tense. Rewrite it in
the future tense. Note that clauses beginning with such conjunctions as
'when', 'if', 'until', and 'unless' are both present and future, and
must not contain the words 'shall' or 'will'. Not that the future of 'can'
may be expressed by 'shall (or will) be able to'.

The rain, snow, and frost attack the surface of the rock. When the outer
surface is worn away a new inner surface is exposed, and that, in its turn, is
attacked and decomposed. Every winter the moisture in the rock freezes into
ice, and this splits the rock until it is ready to fall to pieces. When it rains, if
you are there, you can see the muddy water running down the slope. This
water finds its way into the river. In this way a whole chain of mountains is
carried into the sea. It takes a very long time for a mountain to be carried into
the sea but in the end all mountains become a part of the bottom of the sea.
But unless the rain, snow, and frost first attack the rock, it does not become
decomposed; unless the rock is decomposed it does not turn into mud; unless
it turns into mud it cannot run down the hillsides, and unless it runs down the
hillsides it is not carried into the rivers or into the sea.

(c) SYNTHETIC SENTENCE-BUILDING

This is a form of composition based on the principle of substitution.
The pupil is given a construction-pattern and is required to compose
a number of sentences having the same or a similar grammatical
formula.

Example. Construction-pattern: subject + direct object pronoun +
finite of *avoir* + agreeing past participle.

Sentences composed by the pupil:

> Vous les avez écrit(e)s.
> Vous m'avez vu(e).
> Nous l'avons lu(e).
> Il les a acheté(e)s.

(d) COMPOSITION BY COMPLETION

The pupil is given a number of incomplete sentences—i.e. sentences
with one or more words missing and replaced by dashes or rows of dots.
The pupil chooses what he considers the most suitable words, and
completes the sentences.

5

Example 1

1. The first month of the year is ....
2. December is the .... month of the year.
3. February is not a summer ....; it is a .... month.

Example 2

1. When we write a letter we ....
2. We cannot see the sun during the night, but ....
3. When both the hands of a clock are pointing to twelve ....

Example 3

1. The sun is larger than the moon; therefore the moon is not ....
2. A river is wider than a stream; therefore a stream ....

Example 4

1. J'irais en Afrique si ....
2. J'aurais certainement consenti si ....
3. Il l'aurait proposé, je ....
4. Si j'étais à sa place je ....

Example 5. Write a story by filling in the gaps between the words below:

The house ...... fire, ... upsetting ...... upper storey. In spite of ...... burned to death. The alarm ...... too late to ......; but two children ...... about the hands and face ...... singed ...... on a stretcher ...... and ...... every attention ...... succumbed.

Example 6. Punctuate, putting in capitals where necessary:

He said to one I cannot see why you came here today my son and I are both ill he of malaria and I with a bad headache I told you to come in four five or six days' time yet you take no heed of my request and though I wrote to you more than once not to come you insist on visiting me today what made you choose so unfortunate a moment.

(e) CRITICISM OF FORM

A favourite application of this type of work is to invite the class to criticize or to correct sentences composed by one or more pupils and written by them on the blackboard.

Another variety of this work is to prepare a number of sentences in advance, each containing some error of style or grammar, which the pupils are called upon to correct.

Or the pupils may be called upon to select what they consider to be the better of two alternative renderings (e.g. (a) The English capital is London; (b) The capital of England is London).

(f) CORRECTION OF MIS-STATEMENTS

A particularly interesting form of work. A number of sentences are given, each containing one or more mis-statements. The pupils are called upon to correct them.

> London is the capital of Japan.
> There are eight days in a week.
> A dog has six legs and cannot swim.
> Æsop was an Englishman, and lived in London about 250 years ago.
> The earth is flat, and the sun goes round it.

(g) FRAMING QUESTIONS

The pupils are called upon to frame questions appropriate to answers which are furnished by the textbook.

Examples of Answers	Questions Required
It is *my* book.	Whose book is that?
It's my *book*.	What is that?
I went to the station yesterday.	Who went to the station yesterday?
I went to the *station* yesterday.	Where did you go yesterday?
I went to the station *yesterday*.	When did you go to the station?

(h) EXEMPLIFICATIONS

The pupils are required to form sentences exemplifying various meanings and uses of certain words or forms.

Example 1. Illustrate by simple examples several meanings and uses of the verb 'to get'. Examples:

1. I am going to get my hat. (*Fetch.*)
2. Have you got it? (*Have.*)
3. It is getting cold. (*Become.*)
4. At what time do you get up? (*Rise.*)
5. I must get this mended. (*Cause to be.*)
6. At last I got him to agree. (*Persuade.*)
7. I could not get it out. (*Extract.*)
8. I got there at three o'clock. (*Arrive.*)

Example 2. Give some examples illustrating the gerund. Examples:

   1. *Seeing* is *believing*.
   2. I remember *doing* it.
   3. I can't help *feeling* sorry for him.
   4. I was prevented from *writing*.
   5. I am used to *doing* it.

Stage 5. Vocabulary Extension (Of a duration of, let us say, 300 hours)
We say three hundred hours, but we might have said five hundred or one hundred. For once the major mechanisms have been acquired the only useful grading is vocabulary grading, and the enrichment of vocabulary is as long or as short a process as teacher or pupil cares to make it.

All the processes described in Stage 4 will be continued with texts of increasing difficulty due to increasing vocabulary and also increasing complexity of the thought expressed. Beyond that the work is not so much graded as continuous and cumulative. The student will be given certain units made up of a text (the text of a short story, of a play, of an essay, for example), explanatory introduction (to be given orally or studied outside the classroom), and direct method composition exercises thereon.

In addition to this, opportunities will be given for extensive reading—'extensive' used in a technical sense, as opposed to the 'intensive' reading of the units upon which the composition exercises are based. Care will be taken to ensure that the texts for extensive reading shall be well below the level of difficulty of the texts for intensive reading.

Stage 6. Free Composition, Translation, and Special Studies (Of the duration of the remainder of the student's lifetime)
We feel that by this time our pupils will have come to possess the language 'as speech'. They will not possess the whole language—who does?—they will not possess as much of the language as their teachers, but they will possess it in essentially the same way as their teachers. Now this is a great accomplishment, which it has cost effort, patience, discipline, self-control, time, temper, and money to acquire. It must not be lost. The native goes on possessing his language as speech because he goes on thinking *with* it; some think more, the majority think very much less, but all do *some* sort of thinking with it. Our aim must be now to ensure that this precious possession, the capacity to

think with a foreign language, is not lost. This being the case, a certain measure of the Stage 5 disciplinary work will be continued, continued in the same spirit as 'the daily dozen' are undertaken; the pupils will be keeping fit, fit to think with the foreign language.

(a) FREE COMPOSITION

In view of what has gone on before it is now safe to introduce free composition without fear of the danger of mental translation. At this point no student will be fool enough to go through the long and arduous process involved in mental translation when he has a flood of acoustic images in the foreign language surging into his mind the moment he takes up the pen.

This free composition work will be of such a nature as to prepare him for the compositions required in the examinations for School Leaving Certificates or for university matriculation certificates.

(b) TRANSLATION

The aim will now be to get the pupil to relate the new instrument of thought to the old. For long he has kept them separate and he has come to think new thoughts in the foreign language—thoughts that he has never thought in his own. Moreover, he has thought old thoughts in new ways, unconsciously impregnating himself with the genius of another people, thus getting from his foreign study its greatest mental, and even moral enrichment. But, that the new experience shall bear its fullest fruit, it must be related to the old. Modern studies do not aim at creating dual or treble personalities, but at making personalities doubly and trebly rich. The pupil will now enter upon what is one of the most delightful periods of his language career, the period of thinking successively with two different thought instruments, the period of translating thought, spirit, national genius, into other thought, other spirit, other national genius; the period of *real* translation—the only sort of translation that is not a travesty of the word.

Once again we would point out that his course of study has been an ordered progress. We have not let him speak till he had sounds to speak with; we have not let him read or write till he had words to read or write with; we have not let him do free composition till he had the mechanisms to compose with; and now finally we have not let him translate till he has enough of the foreign language to translate with.

This translation work carried on over a relatively short period will prepare the pupil for the requirements of *thème* and *version* for the School Leaving examinations described above.

(c) A COURSE OF LITERATURE

And so to the things that he can do in, through, with, and about his new possession. He is fit now to study the foreign literature: he can approach it with some understanding of both its spirit and its letter. He will derive from it immense cultural advantages, the greater for the fact that he has approached it by the only honest and scholarly way.

(d) A COURSE OF CONVERSATIONAL BEHAVIOUR

But he may wish to do nothing of the kind—and his wishes should be respected. He may wish to study a more difficult aspect of the language —that of conversational behaviour. He may, for example, wish to know the exact conversational reactions of an average Frenchman to all the situations of daily life, and to be able to produce those reactions himself with an effect of spontaneity. Foreign residence is, of course, indicated, but in its default much can be done by systematized study of the subject. That this is an important accomplishment is unquestionable, and is borne out by Professor H. C. Wyld in his *History of Modern Colloquial English* when he says that if English people of the present day were transported back into the seventeenth century most of them would find it extremely difficult to carry on the simplest kind of decent social intercourse.

We should not know how to greet or to take leave of those we met, how to ask a favour, pay a compliment or send a polite message . . . We could not scold a footman, commend a child, express in appropriate terms admiration for a woman's beauty, or aversion to the opposite quality. We should hesitate every moment how to address the person we were talking to . . . Our innocent impulses of pleasure, approval, dislike, anger, disgust, and so on, would be nipped in the bud for want of words to express them . . . If we . . . insisted on speaking in our own way, we should be made to feel before long that we were outraging every convention and sense of decorum . . . We should appear at once too familiar and too stilted; too prim and too outspoken . . . In any case we should cut a very sorry figure.

Substitute for the two hundred years the different linguistic environment, and we are face to face with similar problems and possibly a similar discomfiture. Not all language-learners require the specialized knowledge that would make them able to deal in a foreign language with the circumstances described. Some do, however, and the advanced language course should give that instruction systematically and scientifically.

(e) A COURSE OF HISTORICAL GRAMMAR AND PHILOLOGY

Another—and possibly equally important—specialist's study in relation to language is that of historical grammar and philology. It is legitimate to suppose that many of those who have manifested an interest in a modern foreign language will wish to know more of its ancient forms and of the development from one to the other. The precise nature of such a course must depend very largely on the purpose for which the knowledge is required. But, in the majority of cases, it is manifest that such studies cannot be undertaken without such a competent knowledge of the modern foreign language as we now presume our pupils to possess.[1]

As to the language in which this course shall be given, on purely academic grounds there would appear to be no particular advantage in giving it in the language which it particularly concerns. Here we shall be guided entirely by the convenience of the professor who gives it and that of the students who take it.

(f) A COURSE OF COMMERCIAL CORRESPONDENCE

We often come across courses in commercial French, commercial German, and the like; but we find upon examining them that they are simply courses in French or German with, at the beginning, *voici le dossier* substituted for *voici la chaise*, and, towards the end, a series of commercial letters. The actual fact seems to be that there is no such thing as commercial French or commercial German as distinct subjects, any more than there is such a thing as legal French or bicycling German; these are merely questions of vocabulary which the possessor of a language as speech can deal with as easily and as rapidly as in his native language. The special forms of commercial correspondence, however, do require a certain amount of special study in a foreign language, as in the mother-tongue. But they cannot be usefully studied without such a competent knowledge of the ordinary forms of the language as we now presume our pupils to possess.

[1] In this connexion see Sweet's *Practical Study of Language*. Reprinted Oxford University Press, 1964, p. 119.

(g) A COURSE OF GENERAL STYLISTICS, INCLUDING VERSIFICATION, PROSODY, AND STYLISTIC VALUES

The greater part of the title of this course is self-explanatory, and requires no particular justification or comment. In its higher aspects it is not the course for the many, but for the gifted or leisured few. The preliminary study of stylistic values, however, will be recommended to all pupils who will have occasion to write the foreign language under a number of varying conditions. Babu English is a grotesque linguistic pleasantry—the perpetual stopgap of the comic papers—but it is none the less representative of a tragedy in which all language-learners share. The grammars have no help to offer us, the dictionaries until now very little. Such classifications of words and expressions as 'slang', 'technical', and 'archaic' are helpful but inadequate. What is required is systematic and scientific classification in every language of what the senior partner in this work has called 'the coloured words and collocations'.

(h) A COURSE OF THE HISTORY AND INSTITUTIONS OF THE PEOPLE WHOSE LANGUAGE HAS BEEN STUDIED

If language for many leads to literature it leads for an equal or perhaps a greater number to a study of the institutions of the people whose language has been learned. Such a course is at once an encouragement to further linguistic study and an intellectual reward for the study made up to the present. No full language course is complete without it, and it may be that where practicable it would be desirable for such a course to be divided into two distinct sections—the one to be given in the pupil's native language at the time when he begins upon his linguistic career; the other, much more thorough and detailed, to be given in the foreign language as an advanced study.

(i) SPECIAL PREPARATION FOR EXAMINATIONS

As Wyatt[1] has aptly put it,

If, then, the teaching is to effect its purpose—of teaching the pupil serviceable English—the examination which is a passport to university and other careers, must co-operate, and not conflict, with the teacher in this endeavour. Unfortunately, this co-operation is not at present secured, and the anomaly exists of a public examination, established to test a candidate's knowledge of English, thwarting the progress of the teaching because it tests something else.

[1] *The Teaching of English in India*, by H. Wyatt. Oxford University Press, 1923.

In other terms, we have been teaching our pupils one subject, where-as they are going to be examined in another. However much we may deplore this, we shall be judged by results, and results in the field of education are all too often simply results in examinations. We may contend that we have achieved a satisfactory linguistic result, but, in point of fact, we have to achieve an examination result. How, then, to satisfy our own linguistic consciences and our pupils' linguistic examiners?

In every School Leaving Certificate examination there are questions on a curious subject which we find some difficulty in defining. It might be called 'comparative grammar' if it were not for the fact that the term seems to suggest a comparison between the grammars of several languages. This examination subject, however, is simply comparison between the grammar of the language learned and that of the pupil's mother-tongue. In a French paper, for example, a candidate will be asked, 'By what construction in French do you render the accusative-infinitive construction in English after verbs of volition?' Now, our pupils who would use *Je veux que vous fassiez cela*, not with the feeling of having achieved something queer, but simply with the feeling of having used the French form naturally, would up to Stage 6 be completely stumped by a question of this kind. We have, then, to provide a course of 'Grammar Translation' for such of our pupils as will submit themselves, and incidentally us, to the judgment of results examinational.

H. V. R. That seems about all we've got to say.

H. E. P. In the present volume at any rate.

H. V. R. Yes, there is probably a lot of amplification to be done, but after all we have done something here in clearing up our own ideas—and perhaps those of some of our readers—as to what this 'Language-Learning Business' is.

H. E. P. Yes, we have made up our minds what a language is: it's a collection—a queerly mixed collection—of symbols, which serve, among other things, as instruments of thought.

H. V. R. And we've made up our minds what learning is: it's this process of *fusing*, fusing the symbols to the things they symbolize.

H. E. P. Yes, and of course the business is to assist and accelerate that fusion. I think in these three sentences we've got the whole thing in a nutshell.

Appendix: Types of Linguistic Symbols

The linguistic symbols of which languages are composed are:
1. *Alogs*, or wordless symbols.
2. *Miologs*, or symbols less than words.
3. *Monologs*, or single-word symbols.
4. *Pliologs*, or compound words.
5. *Collocations*, or successions of words.
6. *Construction-patterns*, or word-moulds.

1. ALOGS, OR WORDLESS SYMBOLS

These are symbols that are neither words, parts of words, nor combinations of words. They are the 'wordless' symbols.

Among these are *word-order* (in English and other languages interrogation is often expressed by word-order alone), significant *stresses* and *tones*, significant *pauses*, and significant *word-omission*.[1]

Many inflected forms are alogistic. The plural of 'sheep' and the past participle of 'put' are examples.

2. MIOLOGS, OR SYMBOLS LESS THAN WORDS

These consist of *inflectional affixes* (e.g. the 's' of 'tables', the 'ed' of 'wanted', the 'ing' of 'waiting', the 'er' of 'shorter', or the 'ge' and the 'en' of 'gefallen'), of *derivational affixes* (e.g. the 'ness' of 'goodness', the 'ation' of 'transformation' or the 'un' of 'unhappy'), and of such symbols as the 'ex' of 'ex-president', the 'vice' of 'vice-chairman', or the 're' of 'rewrite'.

3. MONOLOGS, OR SINGLE-WORD SYMBOLS

The vast majority of linguistic symbols are single or uncompounded words, such as 'cat', 'idea', 'go', 'thing', 'you', 'some', 'black', 'good', 'fortunately', 'on', 'and'.

[1] The absence of 'the' before 'milk' in 'I like milk' fulfils the function of indefinite article. The absence of a subject word in 'Come here' fulfils the function of imperative.

These are the most concrete of all linguistic symbols, and probably most people imagine them to be the only linguistic symbols.

4. PLIOLOGS, OR COMPOUND WORDS

These are intermediate between *monologs* and *collocations*, and run almost insensibly into either category. Typical examples of these are: 'upset', 'overthrow', 'onlooker', 'good-looking', 'motor-car', 'would-be'.

5. COLLOCATIONS, OR SUCCESSIONS OF WORDS

If a succession of words is nothing other than a normal coming-together of words in accordance with the ordinary rules of sentence-building, so that a person knowing the meaning of each of the component words will thereby know the meaning of the succession as a whole, the collocation is said to be regular. Such, for instance, are: 'I went to the station yesterday', 'Give me one of those books', 'Why did you take that?'

If, on the other hand, a collocation contains one or more words having meanings only possible in that collocation or if in other ways the collocation must be learnt as a whole, it is said to be irregular. Such, for instance, are: 'by the way', 'as a matter of fact', 'in the ordinary course', 'to set about', to run away'.

Most teachers and students fail to realize how exceedingly numerous are these irregular collocations.

6. CONSTRUCTION-PATTERNS, OR WORD-MOULDS

The last type of linguistic symbol consists neither of specific words, parts of words, or collocations as such, but of collocations subject to more or less extensive *substitution*. It is not, for instance, that the sentence 'It is impossible for me to do that', as it stands, is a construction-pattern, but it is a representative sentence cast in the mould of the formula: subject + any finite tense of the verb 'to be' + adjectives such as 'possible', 'impossible', 'difficult', 'easy', 'right', 'wrong', 'better', etc., + for + any direct object + any infinitive + any direct object.

It is, then, the totality of sentences that can be cast from such a formula that constitutes this particular construction-pattern.

Among the commoner construction-patterns of English are:

Subject + finite verb + direct object.

Subject + finite of the verb *to be* + predicate.

Among the less common are:

Adverb of the 'in', 'out', 'off' type + subject + finite verb (e.g. 'Off he went!' 'In you go!').

For + the + 'last' or 'past' + expression of number + words such as 'minutes', 'days', 'weeks', etc. (e.g. 'For the last twenty minutes.' 'For the past few years.').

The above, then, is the classification of the linguistic symbols.

The 'things symbolized' (or *symbolendums*, as they may conveniently be called) also need some classification. This is more difficult, for the scheme of classification must differ according to the language in connexion with which it is considered.

All that can be said is that at one end of the scale we find symbolendums having a particular and concrete character, and, at the other, those having a general and abstract character.

Among the former we find those symbolendums which are represented in English by, for example, 'cat', 'sky', 'post-office', 'House of Commons', 'you', 'some', 'a large number of', 'see', 'push', 'overthrow', 'to set about', 'black', 'good-looking', 'pale blue', 'on', 'in front of', 'a few weeks ago', 'and', 'for want of'.

The linguistic symbols standing for symbolendums such as these are considered traditionally to fall within the domain of lexicology, or word-study. We note, indeed, that such symbolendums are usually (but not invariably) symbolized by monologs, pliologs, and collocations (precisely those types of linguistic symbols that are associated with vocabulary rather than with grammar).

Among the examples of symbolendums having a more general and abstract character are those designated in English by such terms as: affirmation, negation, interrogation, exclamation, indicative, imperative, anteriority, futurity, volition, obligation, potentiality, probability, desideration, intensification, concession, causation, subject function, direct object function, indirect object function, etc.

The linguistic symbols by which such abstract conceptions are represented are considered traditionally to fall within the domain of grammar. We note, indeed, that such symbolendums are usually (but not always) symbolized by alogs, miologs, and construction-patterns (precisely those types of linguistic symbols that are associated with grammar).

Were these two categories mutually exclusive, if a sharp line of demarcation could be drawn between them, each might definitely be designated by some clear term; but between the two extremes we find an indefinite number of symbolendums merging imperceptibly into either category. The arrangement differs, too, according to the language. In language A a monolog symbolizes what is symbolized in language B by an alog or a construction-pattern; hence those to whom language A is the mother-tongue tend to look on the thing symbolized as pertaining to the dictionary, while those to whom language B is the mother-tongue look upon it as pertaining to the grammar.

Nevertheless, in the present volume (in the section entitled Stage 4) the symbols standing rather for grammatical than for vocabulary concepts have been called 'mechanisms', and the most frequently occurring (or the most important) of these have been called specially 'major mechanisms', in contradistinction to the less important or 'minor' mechanisms.

Bibliography (1932)

ALGERNON COLEMAN: *The Teaching of Modern Foreign Languages in the United States*. The Macmillan Company, 1929.

L. FAUCETT: *The Teaching of English in the Far East*. Harrap, 1927.

H. FOWLER: *Modern English Usage*. Clarendon Press, 1926.

W. H. FRASER and W. SQUAIR: *Heath's New Practical French Grammar*. Heath, 1922.

C. H. HANDSCHIN: *Methods of Teaching Modern Languages*. World Book Company, 1923.

O. JESPERSEN: *Language: its Nature, Development, and Origin*. Allen and Unwin, 1922.

—— *Mankind, Nation, and Individual from a Linguistic Point of View*. Williams and Norgate, 1925.

—— *A Modern English Grammar*. Allen and Unwin, 1928; Carl and Winter, Heidelberg, 1909–32.

—— *How to Teach a Foreign Language*. Allen and Unwin, 1904.

H. L. MENCKEN: *The American Language*. Knopf, 1919.

H. E. MOORE: *Modernism in Language Teaching*. Heffer, 1925.

C. K. OGDEN and I. A. RICHARDS: *The Meaning of Meaning*. Routledge, 1927.

H. E. PALMER: *A Grammar of Spoken English*. Heffer, 1924.

—— *The Oral Method of Teaching Languages*. Heffer, 1921.

—— *Everyday Sentences in Spoken English*. Heffer, 1922.

H. POUTSMA: *A Grammar of Late Modern English*. Jaschke, 1928.

E. SAPIR: *Language, an Introduction to the Study of Speech*. Harcourt, Brace, 1921.

A. SÈCHEHAYE and C. BALLY: *Cours de linguistique générale*. Payot, 1916.

H. SWEET: *The Practical Study of Languages*. Dent, 1913; Oxford University Press, 1964.

—— *A New English Grammar*. Clarendon Press, 1900.

W. VIËTOR: *Die Sprachunterricht muss umkehren*.

H. WYATT: *The Teaching of English in India*. Oxford University Press, 1923.

H. C. WYLD: *A History of Modern Colloquial English*. Fisher Unwin, 1920.

—— *The Growth of English*. Murray, 1923.

Le Maître Phonétique. Organ of the International Phonetics Association.

Modern Studies. His Majesty's Stationery Office, 1918.

The Modern Language Forum. The Modern Language Association of Southern California, June 1931.

HAROLD E. PALMER: A BIOGRAPHICAL ESSAY

Dorothée Anderson

Acknowledgements

In writing about my father and his scholastic career, I am indebted to my aunt, Miss Dorothea Palmer, for sending me various press cuttings, etc. I would like to thank Mr A. S. Hornby for permission to include extracts from his articles and in this context I am also indebted to the late Professor Daniel Jones. To Dr H. Bongers my thanks are due for allowing me to quote from his thesis and for the list of my father's works. I am most grateful to Sir Vere Redman, not only for permission to include extracts from his article, but for his great help to me generally, so willingly and generously given.

Angmering-on-Sea,   DOROTHÉE ANDERSON
Sussex.
1968.

1. Early Years: England, France, Belgium

Part of the very early years of Harold Edward Palmer, my father, were spent between London, where he was born on 6 March 1877, and a small town in Northants where his father was headmaster of a school. When he was about five, his parents moved to the town of Hythe, on the borders of Romney Marsh, where his father set up a school of his own. It was here that his education began.

Although most of his relatives followed the scholastic profession, his father never really cared for teaching and, having a leaning towards journalism, he gave up the school and founded and edited a local newspaper—the *Hythe Reporter*.

The young Harold then attended a private school in Hythe under the Rev. Betram Winnifrith called 'Prospect House School', and it was at this time that his ability began to emerge, with particular emphasis on languages.

A school report dated Easter 1892, at which time he would be fifteen years old, records his class position as having been first in English, French, History, Geography, Euclid and Reading. He was also first in Divinity, and at one time the suggestion was that he should enter the Church—a suggestion in which he showed no interest; nor did he in those days have any leaning towards the teaching profession. His own preference, I believe, would have been to go on to a university, but his father, having been a French scholar and recipient of the Palmes Académiques from the French Academy, had other ideas. So, in his late teens, he was sent to Boulogne to learn to speak French.

Having a studious father and artistic mother he, himself, combined a fondness of learning with a love of many forms of art. It would seem that in Boulogne most of his time was spent in the Art Gallery sketching and painting in oils. However, his natural aptitude as a linguist was apparent, for he became a proficient French speaker.

On his return to England, he joined the staff of the *Hythe Reporter*, acting as journalist and contributing articles on various subjects.

His father found him to be both an asset—and a problem! His wit would keep breaking out in Gilbertian skits when engaged in reporting on Town Council meetings and his method of reporting in general was, to put it mildly, unorthodox.

About this time, Father became interested in geology and would cycle hundreds of miles, rucksack on back, searching for fossils. On one of these cycling tours he found himself at Felbridge in Sussex, where he admired the lush countryside and took a fancy to the gracious houses there. It was then that he decided that, if the opportunity ever arose, this was where he would like to live, a wish that was fulfilled years later. Geology continued to be of interest to him throughout his life, and in whatever country he found himself, he would go digging for fossils and in this way amassed a considerable collection of rare specimens.

Although Father found life to be full of interest and excitement, he felt that he must break away from work that was leading nowhere. So, in his mid-twenties, feeling cramped and frustrated, he had the urge to go abroad.

Accordingly, in 1902, Father went to the town of Verviers in south-east Belgium where he took up the post of assistant teacher in the École Internationale des Langues Vivantes. There, for the first time, he was introduced to the Berlitz Method. He was trained in the use of the Berlitz technique by witnessing the procedures of the teacher in the English classes and by taking lessons himself in elementary German—a language then unknown to him. This technique was a revelation to him, especially as he had hitherto been in complete ignorance of the Direct Method in any of its forms, and at once he became an enthusiastic admirer of it.

This, then, was his first practical experience of language teaching.

In the following year, Father established his own School of Languages with one or two assistants teaching mainly English and French, and was thus free to use and develop whatever system of teaching he pleased. He explored the possibilities of one method after another, both as teacher and student. He would devise, adopt, modify or reject one plan after another as the result of further research and experience in connexion with many languages—living and artificial.

By this time, he had become fascinated by languages, all languages, his own and other people's, fascinated by the way they worked. He was naturally eager to teach what he had learned and to learn as he taught.

There was a great demand for English among the local people with their large-scale commercial contacts with Britain. He came face to face daily with the problems of teaching English as a foreign language. He learned there two things; first, that the successful teacher *must* keep the interest of his pupils, and secondly, that his teaching must produce fairly rapid results. He began to get results at Verviers mostly out of hard-headed adults, not the captive audience of the classroom, and it is, of course, in such conditions that teaching techniques are really learned—the hard way.

It was here that the Palmer method began to evolve.

An indication of the reputation which, in so short a period, Father had established among these same hard-headed adults is illustrated by the fact that in 1905 a banquet was given in his honour by La Société Polyglotte in Verviers.

In 1904, Father met and married my mother, Elizabeth Purnode, a Belgian possessed of a sweet and placid disposition; it was the contrast in personalities, I think, which made this such a happy partnership during the whole of their married life. Sir Vere Redman who, during his long association with Father, got to know her pretty well, has this to say of her:

Elizabeth, or 'Dees', as H.E.P. used to call her, always seemed to me the ideal wife for an inevitably erratic genius. She was not only gentle and kind; she was also down to earth, practical and, above all, 'unflappable', as the modern jargon has it. She took it for granted that menfolk in general and H.E.P. in particular needed looking after in all the practical business of life such as getting meals, paying bills and serving drinks; that was *her* business. Theirs was to litter the floor with papers, work at all hours and have fits of exultation and depression. They needed comforting and cosseting. I was a marginal beneficiary of these attentions. I appreciated them very much; H.E.P. appreciated them even more.

One of Father's closest friends during the Verviers days was Charles Lemaire, a specialist in the teaching of French as a foreign language. He was deeply impressed by Lemaire's fervour and by the similarity of their views which included not only languages but a love of the same kind of music. As a very little girl, I recall seeing these two enthusiasts together and I knew that the subject of conversation would be either languages or classical music. One thing which stands out clearly in my mind is a phonograph with large horn, reproducing music interspersed with scratching noises to which they would listen with rapt attention. Throughout his life, Father was a great lover of music and in later years collected a considerable number of records of his favourite composers including most of the Gilbert and Sullivan operettas.

Another of his friendships dating from the Verviers days, although in the early stages it was pursued mostly by correspondence, was that with Professor Daniel Jones who was head of the Department of Phonetics at University College, London. In an article which appeared in the Janvier—Juin 1950 edition of *Le Maître Phonétique*, he wrote of Father:

Palmer had a most original and inventive mind. Early on he invented, among other things, a card-index system for helping students to learn languages. Instructions and exercises were printed on one side of each card and keys were printed on the reverse side.

From the first, he made considerable use of phonetics and for some years used a transcription of his own devising. It was a system in which accents were employed after the French fashion for distinguishing shades of vowel sounds. In 1907, he heard for the first time of L'Association Phonétique Internationale, which he joined in July of that year and became a contributor to *Le Maître Phonétique*. With his customary discernment, he saw the superiority of the 'new letter' system over the 'diacritic' system and very soon discarded his own transcription in favour of that of the International Phonetic Association which he thenceforward employed exclusively.

He was also interested in artificial languages and learned both Esperanto and Ido; he considered the latter to be far superior.

Palmer and I corresponded fairly frequently from 1907 onwards, but I never met him until 1912. The meeting was an accidental one on board an Ostend-Dover boat. Seeing my name on a luggage label, he came up to me and we had a memorable talk on phonetics and we struck up a friendship which it has been a privilege to me to enjoy ever since. This meeting confirmed the opinion I had already formed, viz. that he possessed unusual talent for linguistic theory and pedagogy.

My own recollections of Verviers, where I was born, are now somewhat vague, but I do recall that when I was quite young, I could only read and write in phonetic notation. It was not until we spent Christmas Day on one occasion with relatives in England that the transition into traditional spelling took place. We were pulling crackers and I found a motto in one of them. Having asked several people to read it to me without success and being very keen to know what it said, I tried to decipher it myself—and eventually succeeded! I uttered every letter phonetically at first, then got the gist of the word, and traditional spelling soon became my natural form of reading. As one can imagine, Father was very interested in this as it proved his point, viz. that the transition from phonetic notation into traditional spelling could be made when the child was ready.

It was in Verviers that he began to write some of his earlier text-books. These were:

Correspondance Commerciale Anglaise (Verviers, 1906).

Esperanto à l'Usage des Français (Bruges, Witterijck-Deplace, 1907).

The Palmer Method. Elementary French (Hythe, Kent, 1908).

Cours Élémentaire de Correspondance Anglaise (Verviers, 1912).

Manuel d'Anglais Parlé. Méthode Palmer (Verviers, Léon Lacroix, 1913).

Méthode Palmer. La Langue Anglaise (Verviers, 1913).

Nowadays travelling to and from the Continent is considered to be quite the normal thing to do, but in 1912, it was more unusual. For the summer months of that year, Father brought over to England some of his younger Belgian students. My parents were accompanied by a Belgian couple who assisted them in running a large house in Folkestone overlooking Cheriton Park, which was rented for the duration of their stay. A snapshot taken at the time shows a group of twelve students in their early twenties. The stern look on Father's face was no doubt caused by the responsibility he felt towards his students, as they appear to be full of fun and high spirits. This was an ideal arrangement for the students as they were able to continue with their studies of English and also to gain practical experience in speaking the language; they became acquainted at first-hand with the people and habits of this country. Their families considered this to be of value in preparing their sons for their business careers in the coming years. There were many diversions, such as tennis, boating on the Hythe canal and I daresay visits to the theatre, etc. In fact, the whole venture proved so successful that a similar enterprise was repeated the following year.

Then came the 1914–18 war, which altered many things.

The Germans invaded Belgium at the outbreak of hostilities, and Verviers was one of the first towns to be captured. We remained undiscovered under German occupation for six weeks when Father was advised by his friends there to leave because British citizens were being arrested and deported to prison camps. At the time, the frontier into Holland was still open.

One morning, Father rushed home with the news that the frontier was being closed the next day—it was our last chance of escape! The three of us were bundled into an agricultural cart that was leaving immediately to fetch supplies from Holland for the last time. This necessitated abandoning all our possessions. When we arrived in England, we had literally only the things we stood up in—we were truly refugees!

2. University College

Having made a semicircular trip from Verviers via Holland to Ostend, which up to then had not been captured by the Germans, we arrived in Folkestone where my father's parents and sister were living; in this respect we were more fortunate than the majority of refugees.

This, then, was where Father started a new life.

He began by organizing a language school for teaching English to Belgian refugees. As one would expect, many were penniless but those who were better off were able to contribute towards their lessons. Before long, however, he decided to move to London and there he obtained an appointment as French master in a secondary school.

In October 1915, Father was invited by Professor Daniel Jones to deliver a course of lectures at University College on methods of language teaching. These lectures attracted large audiences, mainly of school teachers, and were the forerunners of many other successful courses; in the following year, he was appointed a regular member of the staff. It was about this time that he also became Lecturer in Linguistics at the School of Oriental and African Studies.

Quite early in his teaching career, Father became aware of the importance of the grading of vocabulary and began working out principles of selection. As early as 1915, he gave a lecture on limited vocabulary when, I have been told, he exhibited some well-thought-out word-lists prepared independently of, and probably without knowledge of, any work that was being done by others in this field. This was his customary way of working; he seldom utilized anyone else's results to help him to arrive at his own conclusions.

The field of vocabulary selection was particularly susceptible to the development of pockets of research because individual workers were approaching the problems differently. Much as Father admired the work of these colleagues, he could not always agree with some of their views on vocabulary control. He found it impossible to collaborate with those who were aiming at selections of words which carried the greatest weight of meaning; he was after words with the maximum of actual and potential usability. He did collaborate with some of the workers in the field, however, notably Dr L. Faucett and Dr Michael West, as is shown by Dr Bongers in Section Six of this essay. The results of that collaboration are to be seen in the *Interim Report on Vocabulary Selection* produced by the New York Conference convened in 1934 by the Carnegie Corporation for discussion of the teaching of English as a foreign language.

It was during the University College period that his interest in intonation developed and this again was an interest which remained with him all through his life. His *New Classification of English Tones* (Tokyo 1933) illustrates clearly enough the originality of his thinking on this subject.

On the social side, I recall that it was not unusual to find Father listening attentively to what one was saying only to be interrupted suddenly and asked to repeat a certain utterance several times in order that he might listen to the intonation or the sounds that interested him. This could be a little disconcerting to strangers.

It is now common knowledge that Bernard Shaw's Henry Higgins in *Pygmalion* was based on Henry Sweet. But when I first saw *Pygmalion* and nowadays when I see the stage or film versions of *My Fair Lady*, all the different Henry Higginses remind me of Father, particularly, of course, in the Covent Garden scene; the attentive ear, the hurried transcription, the immediate and exact reproduction of the *tranches de sonorité*, the apparent disregard of every aspect of the person involved except that of the maker of sounds. And I recall again his Gilbertian description of himself in a revue staged in the thirties by the Tokyo Amateur Dramatic Club—'my mission, my ambition, is to be the living model of the perfect phonetician'.

During the years 1917–21 Father wrote his three most important books on methodology. These were *The Scientific Study and Teaching of Languages* (Harrap, 1917, Oxford University Press, 1968); *The Principles of Language Study* (Harrap, 1921, Oxford University Press, 1964); and *The Oral Method of Teaching Languages* (Heffer, 1921).

A Grammar of Spoken English (Heffer) although not published until 1924, was largely written during the University College period (Revised edition, Heffer, 1968). It is a scholarly work, but again it is an eminently practical one. English is seen as a language to be learned rather than learned about and its grammar as a guide to that learning and only as that.

Thereafter, both his teaching and his studies became more formally academic but they never lost their eminently practical character or their originality of approach.

By the early 1920s, then, the academically unqualified teacher had won a place at the top of the academic tree by proven knowledge and achievement in all branches of his subject. Mr A. S. Hornby has this to say of the comprehensiveness of that knowledge in an article which appeared in the January 1950 edition of *English Language Teaching*:

Palmer was a planner. He liked to see his work as a whole, to have the bird's-eye view, and then to examine it in detail. All aspects of a course, its vocabulary, the order of that vocabulary, the syntax, the phonetics and intonation, had to be carefully thought about, decided upon, and then integrated. He was an expert on the visual presentation of material and a master of the analysis that must precede the composition of the sentence pattern and the substitution table. His work on English grammar was marked by a fresh approach. He believed that grammar should be a catalogue of existent phenomena which have come into being in the course of natural linguistic evolution rather than a collection of problems explainable by logic. Like Henry Sweet, for whose work he had a deep admiration and respect, he refused to stretch English in the Procrustean bed of Latin grammar. Grammar, Palmer believed, should be designed so as to provide a set of 'Directions for Use'; and if these directions could be made clearer by throwing overboard worn-out terminology and replacing it with neologisms, Palmer did not hesitate. Conservatism has proved too strong to allow all these neologisms to pass into common currency. But his *Theory of the Twenty-four Anomalous Finites* (Tokyo 1935), even though the finites are now more usually called 'special verbs', has found its way into scores of textbooks and articles during recent years. The theory is one of his most valuable contributions to the study of our grammar mechanism.

I suppose that I was not fully aware at the time of the magnitude of Father's achievement as a practical scholar. I was more aware of incidental characteristics which made him a fascinating companion for leisure time. For instance, histrionics came naturally to him. This helped, of course, to make his lectures popular; he would act out situations to drive a point home and thus bring amusement and relief to the sedate lecture room. But it also made him a source of entertainment in the home. I remember particularly how I used to look forward to the regular short period in the evenings when he would read aloud to me, interpreting the characters in the various stories in so realistic a manner that he made them come alive. In this way, I was introduced to many well-known authors whose works I enjoy to this day. I carried on this practice with my own son, Neil, in later years and I think he enjoyed it, but I never managed to achieve the same vividness and versatility of interpretation as Father.

Looking back now and discussing him with those who knew him best, it seems to me that creative versatility was his most outstanding characteristic. He was always 'up to something or other', much of it related to his special field of study, of course, but quite a lot of it in other fields, too. I recall, for example, that during this period in London, he made a geological model of the Isle of Wight, which he presented to the Department of Geology at University College and which was on display there until it was destroyed by fire. Even in his leisure moments, he had to be creative—to make things.

I am informed by his sister that, as a small boy, Father was taken to a Japanese Exhibition at Earls Court, and immediately became fascinated by all things connected with Japan. He would paint the walls of his den with pictures copied from Japanese screens. No wonder then that when he was invited to go to Japan in 1922 for the purpose of studying and advising upon the teaching of English in that country, he jumped at the opportunity of being able to combine both scientific and artistic interests.

3.   Summer Recess

The family, now including my brother Tristram, born in 1920, followed Father out to Japan in March 1923, which, as it turned out, proved to be a year not to be forgotten by those who were there at that time.

Travel to the Far East in those days was usually by sea via Suez, and the six weeks' voyage was an exciting and enjoyable interlude, seeing *en route*, as we did, many strange and interesting ports for the first time. The disembarkation port was Kobe where of course we were welcomed by Father who immediately whisked us off to view some of the beauty spots before proceeding to Tokyo.

At first we lived in a semi-foreign style house in Koishikawa which Father had rented against our arrival, but it was rather far from the centre of things, so in 1926 we moved to a house in Akasaka Daimachi. This was to be the family home for the next ten years, but mine for only a short period as I was married in February 1927 to Basil, an engineer with the English Electric Co. at Tokyo. These semi-foreign style houses were so called because although they were of similar construction to a Japanese house, wooden with tiled roof, the interior was arranged to enable European style furniture to be accommodated. Thus some rooms were fitted with the traditional *tatami* and others with wooden floors to support heavy furniture not suitable for purely Japanese rooms. Many of these houses were extremely pleasing aesthetically and I remember being fascinated by all the Japanese elements in ours, the sliding partitions (*fusuma*), the inside paper windows (*shoji*) and above all the alcoves (*tokonoma*) with their one hanging scroll (*kakemono*) and a simple flower arrangement, so obviously the focal point in every room which they adorned. But we did not have much time to enjoy these new delights and, be it said, to accustom ourselves to some of the accompanying inconveniences, for in July we were off to the hills.

In order to avoid the extreme heat of the summer months in the cities, it was customary for those who could do so to escape to a suitable resort. Thus, when colleges and schools closed for the summer, we usually left for our sojourn in Karuizawa, a beautiful place in the hills situated about 90 miles north-west of Tokyo, where Father rented a small house for the duration of the holidays.

Karuizawa was a popular meeting place for teachers and others and Father was enabled to continue with discussions on the subject of English teaching in Japan. Teachers from many parts of the country congregated there and he made the most of the opportunity to learn at first hand of their various problems.

During one of these annual visits, the League of Nations happened to be a topical subject of discussion because a four-day conference was being held there under the auspices of the foreign section of the League of Nations Association of Japan. To mark the occasion, Father wrote and produced a Dramatic Revue in four acts entitled 'The League' which, when presented, filled the Karuizawa Auditorium to capacity. The object of this Revue was to convey to the audience, in more or less dramatic form, some idea of the nature, scope and activities of the League of Nations which was in those days—as indeed the United

Nations is today—viewed with a mixture of hope and scepticism. It was written and cast in such a form as to include every range between emotional appeal and broad comedy. Notwithstanding the burlesque and humour which Father introduced, a serious strain ran through the whole of this three-hour show, which was described as an extraordinary presentation. 'The League' was subsequently presented in Tokyo.

During our first summer, at midday on 1 September 1923, the whole Province of Kanto experienced one of the world's severest and most terrifying earthquakes. The focal point turned out to be under the sea off Kamakura Bay, affecting Tokyo, Yokohama and the surrounding countryside for miles including our distant hill resort. It was indeed a strange and frightening sensation to feel the ground under one heave up and down in such an alarming manner. Instinctively, we ran out of the house for fear of it collapsing and burying us alive. Once outside, we all joined hands in the form of an irregular chain because of the risk of falling into crevices or cracks which, on such occasions, not infrequently opened up on the earth's surface. The duration of the quake could not have been more than a matter of seconds—but it seemed far longer. No sooner had we partly recovered than we experienced another acute tremor followed by others. This continued for days but with gradually lessening intensity. During periods of comparative calm, small gatherings of people met to discuss the disaster. It turned out that our community had been isolated from the outside world and this continued for several days. There were many rumours, all of which were pure conjecture. Indeed we heard later that our family had been reported in the English press as having been killed.

That evening, Father decided to climb to a high vantage point in the hills called 'Sunset Point'. On reaching the summit, we could see a huge glow in the direction of Tokyo—and we realized that the city was burning. It was a superb and awe-inspiring sight, filling us with foreboding.

Although our community had not suffered any serious casualty, the days that followed were anxious ones, mainly owing to the lack of authentic news. Father helped to organize a rota and we took turns in meeting unscheduled trains at the small country station. They passed through intermittently, crammed full of people fleeing from the stricken cities—some even lying on the roofs of the carriages. All we could do was to supply the many outstretched hands with such things as rice balls, ice cubes, etc.

It turned out that Tokyo was devastated and still burning—Yokohama had suffered a similar fate and in addition sustained a severe tidal
wave.

Most of the houses in Japan are erected on plinths to give them
flexibility during earthquakes. When eventually we were able to
return to Tokyo, we found, to our relief, that our house was intact
although looking a bit crooked owing to having been partly shaken
off its supports.

4. Palmer's Impact on Japan

A series of articles has been appearing at intervals since November
1964 in the *Asahi Evening News*, Tokyo, on 'Foreign Teachers in
Japan' by Sir Vere Redman. The following are extracts from
No. 44 in the series, which appeared on 7 and 8 April 1966 and the
substance of which has since been reprinted in the February 1967
edition of the *Bulletin of the Japan Society of London*, the December
1966–January 1967 edition of the *K.B.S. Bulletin on Japanese Culture* and
(in Japanese) in the March 1967 edition of *Kokusai Banka*, the last two
published in Tokyo by Kokusai Banka Shinkokai (Society for International Cultural Relations).[1]

In this series, I have referred constantly to Palmer: to his impact on English-
teaching in Japan, to his influence on other teachers, his versatile activities
and his multinational friendships. There can be no doubt that during the
greater part of the fourteen years he was there (1922–1936), he was the most
outstanding figure on the foreign teacher scene.

The reasons for this are that he was a great specialist, in many ways unique
in his speciality, that this speciality was of primary importance to Japan during
the greater part of the time during which he exercised it there, and that he was
possessed of a dynamic personality devoured by enthusiasm and entirely
bereft of cynicism.

It was in a curiously Japanese way that Japan secured his services. This was
brought about not by the Japanese Government authorities but by Kojiro
Matsukata, a member of a distinguished *satsuma samurai* family, who made and
lost two fortunes in business, brought together one of the finest art collections
in the world, including many of the great *ukiyoye* originals which had found
their way to the West in early Meiji days, a collection now housed in the

[1] See also *English Language Teaching*, Vol. xxii, No. 1. October 1967.

museum at Ueno bearing his name, and, almost incidentally, gave Harold Palmer to Japan.

His business interests had brought home to him the importance to the Japanese of a good practical knowledge of the English language. He had been told by many of his compatriots, teachers and students alike, that the methods employed in Japanese schools were old-fashioned and inefficient. When in London on business, he was introduced by Dr Masao Kinoshita, then teaching at the School of Oriental and African Studies, to the 'Daniel Jones gang' at University College. Palmer seemed to the practical Matsukata the most practical and foot-loose member thereof, and so he sought authority from Tokyo to invite this expert to Japan as 'Linguistic Adviser to the Mombusho' (Department of Education) with a view to modernizing English-teaching.

This the Government accorded, albeit with some reluctance, mainly because the proposal was accompanied by an offer to pay the fares of the Palmer family and to guarantee his salary for a period of years. And so Palmer came to Japan as Matsukata's gift to the Mombusho.

The officials did not know quite what to do with him and they can hardly be blamed for that. He would obviously advise reforms in English teaching and reforms are disturbing things, as the Mombusho knew only too well. They would apply to teaching methods and these were pretty firmly under the direction of Professor Yoshisaburo Okakura at the Tokyo Higher Normal School; they would apply to textbooks, and many distinguished teachers of English, directly or indirectly (mostly the latter), and several prominent publishers had a vested interest in these in their existing forms.

Reforms imposed, or even proposed, from on high would upset too many important apple-carts. Matsukata's gift could so easily prove to be a liability!

The solution to the problem finally evolved was as characteristically Japanese as had been the circumstances which had produced the Palmer problem child. Before 'the adviser' could give any advice, a great deal of research had obviously to be done on the nature of the problem. What was required, then, was a research organization under the 'adviser's' direction, operating independently of the Mombusho but under the nominal presidency of its Minister.

There thus was brought into being the Institute for Research in English Teaching. It is fascinating to recall the mixture of motivation in the foundation of that body in May 1923. For many enthusiastic educationists, mostly Japanese but including also a few foreigners, notably the Americans, W. R. F. Stier and Darley Downs, it represented a hope of help with their problems on a national scale. For the vested interests of various kinds and for embarrassed Mombusho officials, it represented a convenient expedient to prevent anything very drastic from happening.

The second group reckoned without the eminence, numbers and enthusiasm of the first and without the energy, adaptability and, above all, the versatile resilience of Palmer himself. Among the eminent enthusiasts was the founder of the Institute, Dr Masataro Sawayanagi, one of Japan's greatest educationists. But some of them were found right in the centre of what had always been believed to be the reactionary camp at the Tokyo Higher Normal School and it was not long before one of the senior teachers of English there, Professor Rinshiro Ishikawa, had joined the Institute Board and invited Palmer to become a regular lecturer at the school itself.

As to the textbook problem, Palmer neither embarrassed nor wasted the time of Mombusho officials with recommendations about existing readers but, after he had visited Middle Schools all over the country, produced the Standard English Readers, a full five-year course, by February 1925. These books got no privileged treatment from the Mombusho from the fact that they were the work of its official adviser. They were published by a relatively small firm, Kaitakusha, then headed by Mr Naoe Naganuma, now head of the famous Naganuma Language School and whose proudest boast was that he had applied Palmer's methods to the teaching of Japanese. They took their place on the market side by side with others all licensed by the Mombusho.

They gained their converts among Japanese Middle School teachers—but not all that many. The same applied to the more advanced texts in the 'English as Speech Series' subsequently produced by Palmer and Institute colleagues. There they were as models for a few enthusiasts to use. There was no pressure on anybody to use them, beyond the pressure of persuasion. Side by side with its textbooks, the Institute poured out a mass of memoranda and research material on every aspect of the English-learning task of immense value to teachers: vocabulary selections, intonation charts, substitution tables and new-type examinations, some of it appearing in special publications and some in the Institute's bilingual monthly *Bulletin*.

In addition to this, the Institute held an annual convention, usually in Tokyo, and organized teacher training courses throughout the country. It also established an educational gramophone record section and issued, in collaboration with the Columbia (Nipponophone) Company, records for English teaching, introducing, for the first time, the famous 'pause device' which has subsequently proved so useful to students.

It can be said, then, that Palmer and the Institute exerted a considerable influence on English teaching in Japan, an influence which has survived, despite the war-time break, to this day. In the exercise of this influence, however, it never really involved the Government, so that the 'reforms' it envisaged were never adopted on an organized national scale.

To that extent, then, those who had seen in its foundation an instrument for preventing anything too drastic from happening were satisfied. On the other hand, the Institute performed another task which none of its founders, with the possible exception of Palmer himself, had ever foreseen. It became a focus for specialized research into the problems of teaching English as a foreign language which was of value wherever English was being taught. In other words, Palmer came to Japan as Linguistic Adviser to the Mombusho; when he left, in 1936, he had become, through the work of the Institute and his work with and through it, linguistic adviser to the whole world where English was being taught as a second language.

It was undoubtedly in Japan that Palmer did his most valuable work in practical terms and his impact on Japan was consequently very great but, as we have seen, in the later phase of his stay there, he was working not only for Japan but also for the whole English-teaching world. Moreover, not all of his impact came from his professional work.

For there was so much of him outside it. He was an enthusiastic and accomplished amateur actor; all right, that went with the job, so to say. He was an ardent supporter of the League of Nations and 'one world' movements generally, an enthusiasm only marginally concerned with linguistics. He was an impassioned amateur geologist, motorist and map-maker, pursuits as remote from linguistics as each from the other.

And he was always having original ideas about these things and many others. Indeed, as has been said of H. G. Wells, 'he could no more help having ideas about things than a dog can help gnawing at a bone'. But the point about all his ideas, all his extra-curricular activities (and these in Japan were many, including the Association of Foreign Teachers, the League of Nations Association, the Tokyo Amateur Dramatic Club and the Asiatic Society of Japan) is that they were pursued not to the detriment, as in the case of so many of us, but as an addition to his main specialized preoccupation.

He was a linguistician first and last but he was also so many other things all the time. He was one of the few great men described in this series.

5. Palmer at Work

Father's methods of work were peculiarly his own—a combination of the coldly systematic and the gustily empirical; I got some personal experience of these fairly early on. Shortly after our arrival in Tokyo, I was sent down to the Furuya School in Osaka for three months to experiment with teaching from some of the Palmer texts. As the pupils in my classes had no knowledge of English, and as I did not speak a word of Japanese, this made an ideal combination for the research work I had been detailed to carry out. On my return to Tokyo, I assisted Father with his work for a short period of time, mainly at home. It was then I came to know his method of working and meticulous care for details.

As a result of much research, the book *English Through Actions* (Tokyo 1925, Longmans Green 1959) was compiled. Having himself been a student of several foreign languages, French, German and Japanese amongst others, and also a teacher of languages, he was able to understand the problems of both student and teacher. The main purpose of this book is for the guidance of the teacher of English as a foreign language. It provides the elements of a Direct Method programme for use in the average classroom of beginners. The material collected is calculated to save the teacher from needless preliminary work and to furnish him with the groundwork of his lessons. In its preparation, every single word was recorded on a card with details of its first and subsequent appearances along with other data. As this work progressed so did references to these cards become more lengthy. A constant review of the known words had to be made and after a certain period of time, they were integrated into the new texts in order that the pupils could become completely familiar with them. In all, it took two years to complete, interspersed with many other activities and commitments.

The idea for *This Language-Learning Business* by Father and Sir Vere Redman emerged on holiday at Atami (a seaside hot-spring resort) in Japan where the Redman and Palmer couples often retreated for weekends from the menfolk's strenuous work in Tokyo. They would compare notes on their teaching experiences in Japan and other parts of the world and on how far apart they were and yet all part of the same business, the business of language-teaching and language-learning. They noted that although engaged in the same business, they had been, in many cases, pursuing completely different ends and indeed concerned with different conceptions of language. 'We ought to try to get some of this sorted out on paper,' said Father, 'and I don't see why we shouldn't set down some of these conversations we have had.'

And so they did. Much of the conversation is recorded pretty well as it occurred. The process of recording was a laborious one, for the work was done before the days of tape recorders and each sentence was written out by hand, mostly by Father. But it was all spoken first. even though there was a good deal of revision as the actual writing went on.

When it came to the letters, the process was much the same. Some of the sentences they contained would be voiced by Father and some by Sir Vere with Father writing busily all the time. They would do a certain amount of revision separately but most of the work was done together and mostly in loud animated voices. Mother has said of their working sessions: 'What a racket they made! It sounded sometimes as if they were having a tremendous row and sometimes as if they were sharing a huge joke.' Sir Vere has added: 'It was essentially a vocal production.'

As a matter of fact, quite a number of Father's productions were vocal at the outset. He liked to 'think aloud', as he called it, when he had a worrying problem. For perhaps several hours on end, he would talk about the pros and cons of this and that until the listener was sometimes quite bewildered. Frequently in the middle of one of these discourses, he would suddenly exclaim: 'I've got it!' and disappear into his study to work things out, sometimes far into the night until the current problem was solved.

At first glance, Father's study would appear to be in a muddle. Books would be open at various places on his desk, spilling over on to the floor surrounding it. Piles of papers in his handwriting would be dotted about the place. But ask him for some point of reference, and he could put his hand on whatever was needed immediately. In later years, he discovered how much more comfortable it was to write on a low Japanese table, squatting on a *zabuton* (a square flat cushion). In this way, he could stretch out for anything he needed without the constant effort of stooping.

From a health point of view, Father was not very robust, particularly in later years. He preferred to go without anything to eat in the middle of the day and to have his main meal in the evenings, but in general he had little interest in food. In the afternoons, he would retire to read and sleep, when the household had of necessity to creep about for fear of disturbing him. Thereafter, completely refreshed, he would delve into work with renewed energy. This was sometimes tiring for those working in close contact with him; so engrossed did he become that he lost all track of time.

Yes, his methods were original in both the English and French senses of the word. They may have annoyed and irritated many people much of the time. But they also delighted and excited many more most of the time.

6.   World Tour and Return to Japan

The following is an extract, slightly adapted, from Dr H. Bongers' thesis, *The History and Principles of Vocabulary Control* (Woerden, Holland, Wocopi, 1947).

In 1931, Palmer felt the desirability of coming into closer contact with those working in the same field as himself, to confer and exchange views with leading exponents of particular schools of thought. To this end, he undertook a world tour. His first stop was Moscow, where he found enthusiasts working and experimenting in various branches of linguistic research not only in connexion with the teaching of English, but also the teaching of Russian in those Soviet Republics in which it was a foreign language. He attended study-circles where the respective merits of the subjective and objective methods of vocabulary control were being debated and where the text-simplifying technique of Dr Michael West was being examined with particular interest.

On his arrival in London, he came into personal contact with Dr West, whose contribution to the problems of vocabulary control had already gained for him an international reputation, chiefly through his New Method Series of readers and composition books.

Palmer next made the acquaintance of Mr C. K. Ogden, who expounded to him the exact nature of the quasi-artificial language that he had named Basic English, and the principles underlying it. Unlike his collaborator, Dr I. A. Richards, Mr Ogden claimed that there was no place for any plan of vocabulary control other than that of Basic. Palmer listened to this exposition with the greatest interest but with very mixed impressions. On the one hand, he found in Mr Ogden one who had no experience in teaching or learning foreign languages, one whose arguments were marked by an amazing naïvity combined with an overbearing and intransigent attitude. On the other hand, he was impressed by the fact that the Basic Vocabulary had been selected subjectively and apparently tested by having been applied to the simplifying of texts. Moreover, was it not Ogden and Richards who, in that epoch-making *The Meaning of Meaning*, had explored the field of theoretical semantics more deeply than anyone since de Saussure? Could it be possible, Palmer asked himself, that, in spite of all appearances to the contrary, Ogden and Richards had hit on the solution of the old and perplexing problem? Was it just conceivable that, with certain modifications, Basic could be made to work? If so, he reflected, he would be prepared to help make it practicable and to experiment with it in classrooms on his return to Japan—and he wrote to Mr Ogden to that effect. His experiments led him to conclude that Basic English was indeed nothing other than its inventors had claimed for it: an artificial language not intended as an approach to Standard English.

Attending the Congress of Linguists at Geneva, he met the veterans Jespersen and Sèchehaye. Shortly after this, he left for America.

Although, in New York, he was unable to meet Professor Thorndike, he spent some weeks conferring with the exponents of the Columbia University school of lexicologists, and noted their propensity to compile statistics almost for the sake of statistics; and his previous impressions were confirmed that they would set out to count without having any clear idea as to precisely what they were counting. Indeed, Palmer's talks and lectures in the United States were devoted largely to urging the need for precise definitions as a pre-requisite for any statistical work, and the place for subjective judgment.

At the Institute of Human Relations (Yale University), he renewed his acquaintance with that linguistic genius, the late Professor Sapir, who approved of Palmer's attitude towards the ultra-subjectivism of Ogden at the one extreme, and the objectivism of those who relied entirely on quantitative statistics.

At Madison, he met Morgan, Cheydleur, Henmon, Purin and others of the 'Wisconsin group' of linguistic statisticians, and discussed with them the various problems of common interest.

At Chicago, he discussed the same problems with Otto Bond and Algernon Coleman; and at Iowa City he met Miss Helen Eddy, one of the most influential advocates of the objective method of vocabulary control.

At Los Angeles, he came into contact with Mr George W. H. Shield, supervisor of modern languages and his staff of teachers of Spanish. Their interpretation of the Reading Approach and vocabulary control seemed to him much more liberal than those that he had met with elsewhere, and he forthwith tried the experiment of learning Spanish according to the principles they advocated. His textbooks were *Beginning Spanish* and *Primeras Lecturas Españolas* by Sparkman and Castillo, who had been influenced by the work of Michael West and the views of Otto Bond, Miss Helen Eddy and Mr Shield. The results of this experiment were set forth in Palmer's Memorandum *On Learning to Read Foreign Languages* (Tokyo 1932). It was then that he noted the factor and importance of cognate words; that to the vocabulary consisting of words deemed to be of the greatest utility (as judged by either the subjective or the objective methods) may be freely added all words common to the language being studied and the mother-tongue of the student.

At Stanford and Berkeley Universities Palmer's views were accepted with enthusiasm. Thus his eight months of conferring and exchanging views with the leading exponents of linguistic methodology came to an end and he returned to Tokyo.

As I look back on Father's fourteen years' stay in Japan, I find that it divides itself pretty distinctly into two halves, each with its own special characteristics, both personal and professional. The first half was a period of pioneering and experiment. He was getting to know Japan and the Japanese set-up as applied to the teaching of English, and it takes fully seven years to do just that. He was breaking new ground in his professional sphere. He was an iconoclast, a revolutionary and an innovator. He was always 'fighting' this, that or the other. By 1929, he had learned a lot and he 'fought' much less. In the second half, the analysis and experimentation still went on but they were less combative and more authoritative. 'I'm not arguing with you; I'm telling you', he seemed to be saying, even on purely Japanese matters. It is to be noted that this authorative accent was increasingly accepted and respected by the Japanese. He became an established institution and as such enjoyed considerable prestige and this not only in academic circles. This increased prestige brought with it increased responsibilities but these were matched by increased anxieties, political, professional and personal. It can be said, then, that, while the second half of his stay was happier than the first, it was certainly no easier.

An example of his prestige was his selection just about the beginning of the second half of his stay to become Tutor in the English language to Prince Chichibu, the eldest of the Emperor's brothers. This was considered a great honour and was accorded to very few Englishmen; I can recall only two, the late Austin William Medley and Professor Edmund Blunden. I understand that, although the meetings with the Prince were formal, they were always pleasant. In those days, motor cars of a distinctive maroon colour were restricted for use by the Imperial family; they were embossed with the usual chrysanthemum crest in gold. At the appointed times, the Imperial car complete with chauffeur would call at our house to drive Father in state to the Palace. Years later, I met Princess Chichibu in London and in the course of a little chat in excellent English, she expressed her gratitude for the great help Father had been to her late husband.

An example of Father's very considerable knowledge of the structure of the Japanese language and linguistic habits is *The Principles of Romanization* (Tokyo, Maruzen, 1930). This monograph is considered by experts on Romanization in general, as well as on the Romanization of Japanese in particular, to be a remarkable book.

I am informed that it came into being under characteristic Palmer impulsions. Father had listened long to the passionate arguments which used to go on (and still do) as to whether Romanized Japanese should be adopted as a national orthography (it has not been yet) and, if so, which of the two systems then in existence should be used. He had friends in all the different camps, including the famous Dr Aisuke Tanakadate, the inventor of one of the systems, who used to enliven the proceedings of the Imperial Diet by presenting in the House of Peers, on the first day of each session, a resolution to the effect that Japan should adopt the Roman alphabet as a national orthography and use his system for this purpose. Father came to the conclusion that most of the argument was at cross purposes. As he wrote in a letter to

Sir Vere Redman, which ran to several pages and included most of the introductory matter to the subsequent monograph: 'These fellows are *all right* to some extent and *all wrong* to some extent because they don't really know what they're arguing about. I *must* tell them.' And that is what the monograph does.

Dr Sanki Ichikawa, who was Professor of English Literature at the then Tokyo Imperial University, now known as the University of Tokyo, contributes the following as a Foreword:

The present book of Mr Palmer's has a twofold interest for us. First, it is an excellent manual of Japanese pronunciation and, written by an English phonetician who has been studying Japanese for many years, full of shrewd remarks and interesting observations. It also contains a brief outline of general phonetics. Secondly—and this is the main purpose for which the book has been written—it is an able and scholarly treatise on the Roman alphabet and on the question of representing the Japanese language through Roman spelling.

Japanese Romanization is a delicate problem associated with bitter controversies, and sage and sagacious people who believe in it theoretically generally avoid using it in practice, saying, as with their religion, that one's belief is one thing and this practical world is another. The existence of the two opposing systems, called in this book the 'Hepburnian' and the 'Nihonshiki', each with followers so uncompromising and antagonistic to each other that of them it might be said that they are 'at daggers drawn', is proving detrimental to the cause of Romanization in general. The author of the present volume, assuming the neutral attitude of a purely 'linguistic technician', endeavours to set forth the merits and demerits of each system and by calling attention to the tripartite division of orthography, transliteration and phonetic notation, attempts to clarify and, if possible, to reconcile the various questions at issue connected with the use of the Roman alphabet. How far the author has succeeded in this remains to be seen, and though I must say I cannot personally agree with him in all his statements and conclusions, still no one can deny that this monograph *does* provide a considerable number of data set forth in such a way that it may be possible for a reader to draw his own conclusions in connexion with more than one vexed question, which it is always our duty to consider without prejudice and partiality.

Examples of the anxieties which accompanied Father's increased responsibilities during the second half of his stay were many and varied. Politically, the period of liberalism was coming to an end, to be replaced gradually by the fanatical nationalism and militarism which

led to the tragedy of 1941. This was obviously an uncongenial atmosphere for work like Father's. One of the manifestations of nationalism
which was particularly discouraging in this sense was the reduction in
the number of hours devoted to English in the middle school curricula.

On the other hand, the Institute had more and more research to
do and less money with which to do it. The Ministry of Education
grant was none too adequate and in a currency sadly depreciated
since the country went off gold in December 1931. The result was that
the Institute always seemed to be working on a shoe-string. In fact, I
recollect that Father and some of his friends made personal loans to
the Institute in the form of 'promissory notes' to tide things over, all
of which, it should be added, were repaid.

Finally, it remains to be said that all this was not without its effect
on Father's personal finances. Royalties on books published abroad
were diminishing because an ever-increasing amount of his publishing
was being done in Japan (as can be clearly seen in the appended list
of his publications) where nearly all his royalties went to the Institute.
The Ministry had taken over from Mr Matsukata responsibility for
the whole of his official salary as Linguistic Adviser, but this was losing
much of its real value in view of inflation in Japan.

And yet, as I say, I think he was happy, despite all his anxieties
because he really enjoyed the challenge they offered. I have already
mentioned that creative versatility was perhaps Father's most outstanding characteristic. He was always avid for new experiences,
intellectual and otherwise; his imagination would take great leaps
which often carried him into fields outside his speciality and away from
any consideration of personal advantage, financial or academic. All
this came out in Japan more perhaps than anywhere else because the
range of interests there was wider, and because the Japanese themselves
are attracted by exuberant personalities, in spite of, or perhaps because
of, not producing many such themselves. In fact, he revelled in all his
experiences in Japan.

And, in a way, the Japanese revelled in him. His dynamism sometimes frightened them, his histrionics shocked some of them, but his
enormous capacity for hard work and original research inspired them
to carry on with his work with the result that the Institute for Research
in English Teaching, now known as the Institute for Research in
Language Teaching, is active to this day. Above all, they came
to admire what they called his 'sincerity', his wholehearted self-
identification with the job in hand.

And so they wished to do honour to this worthy scholar in a way which would give him the greatest satisfaction. In 1935, the Tokyo Imperial University conferred upon him the degree of Doctor of Literature, characteristically not honorary but specifically in recognition of his original research and scientific study contained in *A Grammar of Spoken English*, *English Intonation* and *The Principles of Romanization*.

By this time, he had been in Japan for thirteen years and he was fifty-eight years old. He began to think, as Mother had been thinking since 1931, when the Manchurian Incident occurred and the political situation in Japan began seriously to deteriorate, about where he would like to spend his remaining years. There was something to be said for staying in Japan and carrying on with the work of the Institute which was now of value wherever in the world English was being taught as a second language. But, as Sir Vere Redman has pointed out earlier in these pages, this value was more appreciated outside Japan than in it. Moreover, with the increasing antipathy towards foreigners in Japan, it was becoming more difficult for the work of the Institute to be carried on in that country. Its research workers were as ardent as ever, but the general public and not a few officials were increasingly less sympathetic to an institution concerned with a foreign language and headed by a foreigner. There was, then, a great deal to be said, as far as Father was concerned, for getting out in order to pursue his task in a more congenial atmosphere, from his own, the general and even the Institute's point of view.

In 1935 a suitable opportunity came to do so. As I have already mentioned, the *Interim Report on Vocabulary Selection* was produced as the result of the New York Conference convened in 1934. In the following year, the Conference met again, this time in London, to consider the report and to make arrangements for a tentative Word List. While in London, Father was approached by the publishers, Longmans Green, with an offer to become an adviser on linguistic problems and a writer of books. Father asked his prospective employers what he would have to do in the new job and received the reply: 'Well, just go on being Palmer in England instead of in Japan'.

And so he did. On his return to Japan, he made all the arrangements for the Institute to carry on under the directorship of Professor Rintaro Ishikawa with Mr A. S. Hornby acting as adviser on research and editor of the *Bulletin*, and he finally left Japan in 1936, receiving farewell tributes from all over the country.

7. Felbridge

It was in this year, 1936, that Father was able to acquire a charming house in Felbridge, Sussex, with three acres of land, most of it woodland. This, then, was where, so many years ago, he had hoped to come and live one day.

It was also a happy reunion for the family. Tristram, my brother, had been at school in England for several years by then and as Father was naturally fascinated by the problems and promises of his education, he welcomed the opportunity of being near at hand in order to watch his progress. Tristram had inherited Father's love of classical music and indeed wanted to make this his career. As we, my husband, my son Neil and I, had returned to England the previous year from Shanghai where we had been for the last three years, the family was together once more in the same country. In this happy mood and in these pleasant country surroundings, Father at once devoted his energies to writing further books, mostly designed for foreign learners of English.

As far back as 1912, he had compiled a list of English words, mostly structural, which were generally found to give the most trouble to foreign students, and this formed the nucleus for *A Grammar of English Words* (Longmans Green, 1938). Like a dictionary, it is a collection of words in alphabetical order, but unlike a dictionary, it gives the grammar of each word in detail; it is a *grammar of words*. In 1962 the Central Office of Information decided to include it in their Low-Priced Books Scheme so that it could be made available to people overseas at a price they could afford to pay.

The New Method Grammar (Longmans Green, 1938) is another book which Father wrote about this time. It is written for younger students of English as a foreign language. It is written in English for it is not assumed that the students are ignorant of that language. In general, the book follows the lines of traditional grammar and the terminology with which most teachers are familiar. It deals with the grammar of *classes of words* not with the grammar of *individual words*. The book is looked upon simply as a series of definite instructions as to how to build up English sentences in the manner of those who use English as their mother-tongue.

Father was very keen on introducing charts and diagrams to demonstrate the whole aspect of the particular subject under review. Indeed a number of his books contain such material and a good example of this feature is given in the appendix of *The New Method Grammar*.

It takes the form of a syntactic railway system, viz. sentence construction.

Having at this time more leisure at his disposal to indulge in ideas, hobbies and experiments, Father decided to construct a practical plan of his syntactic railway system in part of the grounds of his property. This involved several months of enjoyable work. He would collect boulders, stones, etc., for placing in strategic positions to form hills in miniature—excavate soil to represent valleys and so forth. Junctions and stations were installed at the appropriate places and as much of the natural terrain as possible utilized to make the whole appear in the form of a large landscape. If a simple sentence were needed, it would necessitate following the main line and picking up one of a number of words at various stations. Or additional words could be introduced by diverting the train on to various lines by means of the appropriate junctions according to the part of sentence needed. This offered innumerable sentences built up in an interesting and amusing manner. It was one of Father's proud achievements and all visitors were invited to inspect his syntax garden for a demonstration of its workings.

The next and last important contribution Father made to the teaching of English as a foreign language is *The International English Course* (Evans Bros., 1944, Oxford University Press, 1965) considered to be his crowning achievement as a textbook writer. As a result of long periods of research, he had acquired a 'vocabulary sense' which enabled him to determine with little hesitation the relative utility of any word or expression, and which of these should be included in or excluded from any textbook at any stage. Originally it was printed in separate bilingual editions for Spanish, French, Italian, Dutch, Czech and Polish students. It is intended for those students who already have some knowledge of English, but need a rapid revision course with the emphasis on conversational English. Its most interesting feature is the systematic presentation of the material in the form of substitution tables, the possibilities of which were first demonstrated by him in his book *100 Substitution Tables* (Heffer, 1916).

When he left Japan, his many friends presented Father with a full-size Japanese room as a memento, to be shipped after he had found a suitable house. One of the unusual features of the Felbridge property consisted of a large loggia which made it ideal for the accommodation of the Japanese room. So, the correct dimensions were supplied and in due course the room was shipped to England all ready for assembly;

it turned out to be correct in every detail. Three sides of the loggia
had glass sliding-panels which, when necessary, could be rolled right
round to the back wall thus allowing an open vista to the garden.
This was where Father worked during the warmer months. Many
years later, the Japanese room was presented to the British Museum
where, as far as I know, it is still in cold storage. The Keeper of
Oriental Antiquities informed me that it would be installed with a
plaque naming Father as the donor when an extension was built to
the existing Museum. I am still hopeful that one day it will be on
display.

The art of *Bonkei* (miniature Japanese landscape gardens on trays)
was a hobby which fascinated Father. He also became interested in
archery, and having plenty of ground in which to spread himself, he
erected a large target. The idea for this recreation was sparked off by
the fact that the bows and arrows brought from Japan were of unusually
fine craftsmanship and with practice could be used with considerable
accuracy. Many happy hours were spent in this way.

Then in 1939 the Second World War came.

Father's activities were devoted to the national effort in so far as it
was possible for him to do so. Apart from his air-raid warden duties,
he devised and introduced several ingenious charts, the outstanding
features being instant reference and scientific pictorial method of
memorizing. These were *First Aid Memory Chart*, *Home Nursing Memory
Chart*, both approved by the St John Ambulance Association, and
A.R.P.[1] *Gas Chart* showing correct procedure in case of casualties from
gas attacks. All these were published by Memory Charts Ltd., London,
together with *Morse Memory Book*, a simplified method in booklet
form for all learners of post-office telegraphy, radio, lamp or flag
signalling.

Textbooks at this time included a *French-English Conversation Dictionary*,
Speak and Understand French (Heffer, 1940) produced specifically for the
British Expeditionary Force.

His only son joined the Royal Air Force and was subsequently
promoted to bomber pilot. As such, he and his crew carried out many
hazardous tours of duty, but in July 1942, he was killed. Father never
really recovered from this shock and from then on his health
deteriorated.

During 1944, he was invited by the British Council to give a series

[1] ARP: Air Raid Precautions.

of lectures in South America. Although he was not well, the doctors and his family felt that a tour of this kind would be beneficial with its complete change of environment. At this time, Mr Ronald Mackin was Director of Studies in the Instituto Cultural Anglo-Uruguayo in Montevideo, where they met for the first time. He tells me that Father gave brilliant lectures but was unable to complete the tour owing to ill-health; and in fact he returned to England a very sick man.

Father collapsed suddenly on 16 November 1949 in his study, surrounded by his beloved books, where I know he would have wished to be. He once said to me: 'I feel a bit lonely sometimes in my field of work.' He would have been overjoyed had he known that all his hard work and research continued to be of use in the English teaching world of today.

List of Harold E. Palmer's Works

The following list is an amended version of that to be found in Dr H. Bongers' thesis *The History and Principles of Vocabulary Control*. Woerden (Holland), Wocopi, 1947.

Abbreviations:
BIRET   *The Bulletin of the Institute for Research in English Teaching.*
IRET   The Institute for Research in English Teaching.

Major Works
A Grammar of Spoken English. Cambridge, Heffer, 1924. Revised edition by Palmer and F. G. Blandford, Cambridge, Heffer, 1939. Revised edition by R. Kingdon, Cambridge, Heffer, 1968.
The Oral Method of Teaching Languages. Cambridge, Heffer, 1921.
The Principles of Language-Study. London, Harrap, 1922. Reissued in the series *Language and Language Learning*, London, Oxford University Press, 1964.
The Principles of Language-Study. Japanese edition. Tokyo, 1923. Also New York, World Book Co.
The Principles of Romanization. Maruzen, Tokyo, 1930. Jap. edn., Tokyo, 1930.
The Scientific Study and Teaching of Languages. London, Harrap, 1917. Reissued in a new edition (edited by D. Harper) in the series *Language and Language Learning*, London, Oxford University Press, 1968.
and H. Vere Redman—*This Language-Learning Business.* London, Harrap, 1932. Also New York, World Book Co., 1932. Reissued in a new edition in the series *Language and Language Learning*, London, Oxford University Press, 1969.

Lexicology

English-French Phraseological Dictionary. London, Evans Bros., 1943–44.
Essay in Lexicology. Tokyo, IRET, 1934.
A Grammar of English Words. London, Longmans, Green and Co. Ltd., 1938.
Also Tokyo, Senjo Publishing Co., 1958.
Specimen Pages of a New Type Dictionary. Tokyo, IRET, 1932.
The Thorndike Junior Dictionary. Revised and edited by P. B. Ballard and Palmer. London, University of London Press, 1947.

Vocabulary Selection

A 600-Word Vocabulary for Story-Telling Purposes. Tokyo, IRET, 1932.
Committee on Vocabulary Selection (Palmer, L. Faucett, E. L. Thorndike and M. West)—*Interim Report on Vocabulary Selection*. London, King and Son, 1936.
Interim Report on Vocabulary Selection. Tokyo, IRET, 1930.
Second Interim Report on English Collocations. Tokyo, IRET, 1933. (First Report not available.)
Second Interim Report on Vocabulary Selection. Tokyo, IRET, 1931.
The First 500 English Words of Most Frequent Occurrence. Tokyo, IRET, 1931.
The Second 500 English Words of Most Frequent Occurrence. Tokyo, IRET, 1931.
The First 600 English Words for a Classroom Vocabulary. Tokyo, IRET.
and A. S. Hornby—*Thousand-Word English: what it is and what can be done with it*. London, Harrap, 1937.
and M. West—'Discussion of Word Frequency', *Modern Languages* Vol. 18 No. 3. London, 1937.
'Our Word List', *BIRET*, No. 82. Tokyo, IRET, 1932.
'The Testing of the Word Lists', *BIRET*, No. 85. Tokyo, IRET, 1932.

Phonetics and Tonetics

and J. V. Martin, and F. G. Blandford—*Dictionary of English Pronunciation with American Variants*. Cambridge, Heffer, 1926. Second edition 1929.
and J. V. Martin—*Documents of English Phonetic Notation*. Tokyo, IRET, 1925.
English Intonation with Systematic Exercises. Cambridge, Heffer, 1922.
and J. V. Martin—*English Phonetic Diagrams*. Tokyo, IRET, 1926.
and F. G. Blandford—*English Pronunciation through Questions and Answers*. Cambridge, Heffer, 1928.
Everyday Sentences in Spoken English. With Phonetic Transcriptions and Intonation Marks. Cambridge, Heffer, 1922. Fifth edition, revised by Palmer and F. G. Blandford, 1935.
A First Course of English Phonetics. Cambridge, Heffer, 1917.
and Dorothée Palmer—*The Mollusc* by H. H. Davies. Annotated Phonetic Edition with Tone-Marks. Cambridge, Heffer, 1929.
A New Classification of English Tones. Tokyo, IRET, 1933.

Principles of English Phonetic Notation. Tokyo, IRET, 1925.

Progressive Exercises in the English Phones. Tokyo, IRET, 1925.

Some Specimens of English Phonetic Transcription. Tokyo, IRET, 1925.

What is Phonetics? London, International Phonetic Association, second edition 1920.

Concerning Pronunciation. Tokyo, IRET, 1925.

50 Gramophone Records plus *Texts with Phonetic Transcriptions and Intonation Marks.* Tokyo, The Columbia Company of Japan.

Textbooks

The B.E.F. Dictionary—A French-English Conversation Dictionary—Speak and Understand French. Cambridge, Heffer, 1940.

Cartes Palmer. Collection A. Verviers, 1906.

Cartes Palmer. Collection B. Verviers, 1907.

Colloquial English, Part 1: 100 Substitution Tables (with Phonetic Transcriptions). Cambridge, Heffer, first edition 1916, second edition 1921, third edition 1923.

and C. Motte—*Colloquial French. Substitution Tables.* Cambridge, Heffer, 1916.

Correspondance Commerciale Anglaise. Verviers, 1906.

Cours Elémentaire de Correspondance Anglaise. Verviers, 1912.

English for Children. Tokyo, IRET, 1927.

and Dorothée Palmer—*English through Actions.* Tokyo, IRET, 1925. Reissued, London, Longmans, Green and Co. Ltd., 1959.

English through Questions and Answers, 4 volumes. Tokyo, IRET, 1930.

Esperanto à l'Usage des Français. Bruges, Witterijck-Deplace, 1907.

The First Six Weeks of English. Tokyo, IRET, 1934.

and E. K. Venables—*Graded Exercises in English Composition*, 6 volumes plus *Keys.* Tokyo, IRET, 1927.

The International English Course. Italian, French, Dutch, Spanish, Polish, and Czech editions. London, Evans Bros., 1944. Spanish version (*Curso Internacional de Inglés*) reissued in the series *Language and Language Learning*, London, Oxford University Press, 1965.

Manuel d'Anglais Parlé. Méthode Palmer. Verviers, Léon Lacroix, 1913.

and Naganuma— *Mechanism Grammar (English); Mechanism Grammar (Japanese)*, with book of *Exercises.* Tokyo, Kaitakusha, 1924.

Méthode Palmer. La Langue Anglaise. Verviers, second edition 1915.

New English Course, 5 volumes. Edited by J. Wilson. London, Longmans, Green and Co. Ltd., 1952.

New Method English Course for West Africa. London, Longmans, Green and Co. Ltd., 1942.

The New Method English Practice Books, 3 volumes plus *Teacher's Handbooks.* London, Longmans, Green and Co. Ltd., 1939. Second edition 1960.

The New Method Grammar. London, Longmans, Green and Co. Ltd., 1938.

The Palmer Method. Elementary French. Hythe (Kent), *Reporter* Office, 1908.

Premier Livre de Français, 2 volumes plus *Teacher's Handbooks*. London, Longmans, Green and Co. Ltd., 1939.

Sequential Series: Questions; Sequential Series: Answers. Tokyo, IRET, 1923.

Systematic Exercises in English Sentence Building. Substitution Tables, 2 volumes. Tokyo, IRET, 1924–5.

The Teaching of English to Soldiers (in West Africa). London, Longmans, Green and Co. Ltd., 1940.

The Teaching of Oral English. London, Longmans, Green and Co. Ltd., 1940.

The Technique of Question Answering. Tokyo, IRET, 1931.

Cours de Français: Nouvelle Méthode, 3 volumes. London, Longmans, Green and Co. Ltd., 1939–48.

Readers

and M. West—*Egyptian Reader*, 3 volumes. London, Longmans, Green and Co. Ltd., 1942.

English as Speech Series: The Adventures of the Three Students; Mrs Thisleton's Princess; Comical Correspondence. Tokyo, IRET, 1931.

The First Six Weeks of English Reading. Tokyo, IRET, 1934.

Longmans' Simplified English Series: A Journey to the Centre of the Earth, 1938; *Round the World in Eighty Days*, 1937. London, Longmans, Green and Co. Ltd.

New Method Readers for African Students: Primer (Pupil's Book and *Teacher's Book); Reader*, 3 volumes plus *Teacher's Supplement*. London, Longmans, Green and Co. Ltd.

New Method Readers for Egyptian Students, 4 volumes. Longmans, Green and Co. Ltd.

Simplified English for Side Reading: Dr Jekyll and Mr Hyde; The Gold Bug, 1932; *Treasure Island*, 1935; (3,000-word vocabulary). *The Gorgon's Head; Pandora and the Box;* (600-word vocabulary). Tokyo, IRET.

Standard English Reader for Beginners, 10 volumes I–V (1 and 2). Tokyo, IRET, 1925.

Standard English Reader for Beginners. Phonetic Edition. Tokyo, IRET, 1925.

and E. K. Venables, and A. S. Hornby—*Standard English Reader for Girls*, 5 volumes. Tokyo, IRET, 1934.

Abridged Standard Readers, 5 volumes. Tokyo, IRET.

Thousand-Word English Series: Aesop's Fables; Boscobel, 2 volumes; *The Deerslayer; Four Tales from Shakespeare; Stories from Robin Hood; Three Tales from Hawthorne*. London, Harrap. Republished in *Plain English Library*. London, Evans Bros.

Other Articles, Leaflets and Booklets

Classroom Procedures and Devices. Tokyo, IRET, 1927.

The Clean Stroke. Tokyo, IRET.

Conversational English and How to Learn it. Tokyo, Kaitakusha.

English Article-Usage. Tokyo, IRET. Also in *English Language Teaching*, Vol. II, No. 3 (November, 1947) and reprinted in *E.L.T. Selections 1.* London, Oxford University Press, 1967.

English Plain and Coloured. Tokyo, IRET.

The Five Speech-Learning Habits, a Paper. Tokyo, IRET, 1933.

The Five Speech-Learning Habits, a Comprehensive Questionnaire. Tokyo, IRET, 1933.

Foreign Language Teaching: Past, Present and Future. Buenos Aires, reprinted from *Overseas Education*, 1944.

Glossary of Technical Terms. Tokyo, IRET.

The Grading and Simplifying of Literary Material. Tokyo, IRET, 1932.

Memorandum on Problems of English Teaching in the Light of a New Theory. Tokyo, IRET, 1924.

Memorandum on Problems of English Teaching in the Light of a New Theory. Japanese translation. Tokyo, IRET, 1924.

The New Type Examination. Tokyo, IRET, second edition, 1928.

The New Type Objective Examination for Proficiency in Teaching English. Special Subject: the 5 Speech-Learning Habits. Tokyo, IRET, 1934.

The New Type Objective Examination for Proficiency in Teaching English. Special Subject: the 24 Anomalous Finites. Tokyo, IRET, 1934.

The Noun Complex, with Diagrams. Tokyo, IRET.

On Learning to Read Foreign Languages. Tokyo, IRET, 1932.

On What Day? Tokyo, IRET.

'The Oral and Direct Methods as an Initiation into Reading', *Modern Languages Forum*, Vol. 17, No. 2. Los Angles, 1932.

'The Preliminary Stage', *BIRET*, No. 86. Tokyo, IRET, 1932.

'The Process of Language Learning in a Nutshell', *BIRET*, No. 82. Tokyo, IRET, 1932.

Pupil's Manual of Questions and Answers. Tokyo, IRET.

The Reader System. Tokyo, IRET.

The Reformed English Teaching in Middle Grade Schools. Tokyo, IRET, 1924.

Report on Research Activities 1928–29. Tokyo, IRET, 1929.

The Right Word. Tokyo, IRET, 1926.

'Sentences Worth Memorizing', *BIRET*, No. 91. Tokyo, IRET, 1933.

The Solitary Reaper. A Study in Stylistic Values. Tokyo, IRET.

Some Notes on Construction-Patterns. Tokyo, IRET, 1931.

Specimens of English Construction-Patterns. Based on the General Synoptic Chart showing the Syntax of the English Sentence. Tokyo, IRET, 1934.

A Study in Construction-Patterns. Tokyo, IRET, 1931.

Synoptic Chart Showing the Various Functions and Uses of the Preposition 'at'. Tokyo, IRET, 1930.

The Teaching of English in Japan. Tokyo, IRET.

'Text-Grading and Linguistic Symbols', *BIRET*, No. 82. Tokyo, IRET, 1932.

' "That Will Come in Handy" ', *English Language Teaching*, Vol. I, No. 5 (March, 1947) and reprinted in *E.L.T. Selections 1*. London, Oxford University Press, 1967.

The Theory of the English Article. Tokyo, IRET, 1935.

The Theory of the 24 Anomalous Finites. Tokyo, IRET, 1935.

and Spencer Kennard—*Thinking in English: 11 lessons in Mental Alertness*. Tokyo, IRET.

To the Japanese Students of English, Tokyo, IRET.

'The Twofold Nature of Language and Language Study: A System and a Mode of Behaviour', *BIRET*, No. 141. Tokyo, IRET, 1938.

What to Do and What Not to Do: Advice to Teachers Using the Reformed Methods. Tokyo, IRET, 1935.

When is an Adjective not an Adjective? Tokyo, IRET.